THE
CHRIST
CURE

10 Biblical Ways to Heal from Trauma, Tragedy, and PTSD

TIM MURPHY, Ph.D.

Humanix Books

www.humanixbooks.com

To Nanette

Contents

Part Three: Six Steps to STAY Healthy

10 Biblical Ways to Heal from Trauma, Tragedy, and PTSD

The Steps to Healing:

Step #1—Build Your Own Resilience

Step #2—Arm Your Resistance

Step #3—Embrace Your Recovery

Step #4—Accept Your Renewal

The Steps to Sustained Healing:

Step #5—Get Fit

Step #6—Strengthen Your Attitude

Step #7—Get Enough Sleep

Step #8—Train Your Mind

Step #9—Eat Healthy

Step #10—Learn to Relax

Author's Note

The Monte Cassino Abbey, a monastery in Italy, was founded in 529 CE. It was attacked, sacked, and abandoned in 570; rebuilt; and in 883 sacked and abandoned again. In 1349, it was destroyed by an earthquake, rebuilt, and then sacked by French troops during the French revolution in 1799. In World War II, it was bombed to rubble.

Over the centuries, each time it was destroyed, it was rebuilt bigger and stronger than before.

The Latin motto of the Abbey is *Succisa Virescit,* which means "having been cut down, it grows back green." Similarly, Isaiah 11:1 and Job 14:7–9 write of a cut-down tree that will come back stronger, and Isaiah 18:5 and John 15:2 remind us pruning the grapevine results in a more fruitful harvest.

Your life and my life are much like that, for whenever we are cut down, we can rebuild, stronger than we were before.

That is the meaning behind the crest representing my counseling practice. A cut tree fiercely and defiantly growing upward, nourished by the four roots of heart, mind, strength, and spirit.

—Tim Murphy, Ph.D.

Preface

Iawoke soaked in sweat. My heart pounded from emotional overload as my mind raced with memories of every mistake, of every wrong, and of everyone I had ever hurt.

In that moment, accomplishments meant nothing. Successes felt meaningless. Only the failures remained.

Maybe you've been there as well.

For me, I was totally and completely overwhelmed with shame, guilt, self-loathing, and anger at myself and my world. I was so terribly alone. I just wanted to remain isolated from the world, curled up in a fetal position in bed, sobbing quietly so no one would hear me. I did not want to eat or sleep or talk to anyone. I welcomed pain as deserved punishment.

With neither the energy nor desire to get up, I drifted in and out of sleep as my soul ran out of gas.

That morning, with light coming through the drawn window blinds, I felt disappointed to still be alive. Another day meant dealing with my misery. It meant continuing my lifelong battle with self-doubt and self-contempt, relationships kept at arm's length while outwardly appearing successful. I had sought the wrong kind of escape outside of my marriage and got involved where I should not have. It blew up in a scandal that led to me resigning my position as a Member of Congress.

The downward crash was fast and painful. One day I was getting praise for public policy achievements and my work to change mental health treatment in America. The next, I was the butt of jokes in late-night opening monologues.

But no one hated me more than I did.

This went on for weeks. One friend told me it would be better to get up and try to rebuild my life. I wasn't sure about that. A few friends, even complete strangers, called or reached out to tell me the same. I refused to listen for a while, but, thank God, they persisted.

I don't remember exactly when it happened, but at some point I realized that despite my pain and shame, life was not hopeless.

Others have had much, much worse trauma and yet emerged the stronger for it. I've seen it. I've witnessed it. And I wanted that for me.

It still took me a long time to reach that conclusion. When we are emotionally overwhelmed, we magnify the bad and are blind to the good. Shame is devious that way.

What's more, I found that the higher you are when you fall, the bigger the crater you make when you hit bottom! And it's very tough to climb out of your own crater.

If you have fallen, if your life has been smashed by trauma, you know what it feels like. But I assure you, no matter how bad the pain, you can fight and scrape your way out.

Join me.

Let's do this together.

Bible Translation Abbreviations

ASV: American Standard Version
BSB: Berean Study Bible
CEV: Contemporary English Version
D-R: Douay Rheims
ESV: English Standard Version
GNT: Good News Translation
KJV: King James Version
NASB New American Standard Bible
NAB: New American Bible
NABRE: New American Bible Revised Edition
NCV: New Century Version
NIV: New International Version
NKJV: New King James Version
NLT: New Living Translation
NRSV: New Revised Standard Version
NRSVA: New Revised Standard Version Anglican
NRSVCE: New Revised Standard Version Catholic Edition

Introduction

From my own humbling experiences, and from the painful experiences that trauma survivors have shared with me over many years as a psychologist and friend, I have learned one supremely important lesson:

> You can survive trauma.

Whether the trauma is external or self-inflicted, you can survive it! Don't let anyone, yourself included, tell you otherwise.

I'm not saying it's easy. Not at all. This may very well be the toughest work you will ever do, but the destination is worth the effort. This is a fight to survive or die, and your response must be strong and urgent.

This is a battle, but victory is yours.

WE ALL HURT

Trauma is everywhere. It may be a life-threatening incident or an overwhelming emotional crisis. It may be directed at you, or you may happen to be a witness. It can be a single intense event or prolonged stress lasting months or years.

About 70 percent of American adults have encountered trauma at some time in their lives. That's around 230 million people.

Most likely, your name is on that list.

Of those people, about 20 percent or 46 million people will develop temporary post-traumatic stress or suffer long-term Post Traumatic Stress Disorder (PTSD) with all its crippling anxiety, nightmares, flashbacks, avoidance, and disability.

There are three different types of trauma:

1. **Random and unavoidable:** These are the sudden, unexpected events totally outside of your control. Maybe you were in or witnessed a car accident, murder, assault, weather disaster, fire, or kidnapping. It can also include being diagnosed with a life-threatening illness or having a child requiring years of medical treatment. Compassion from others can help, but it will not erase the pain. The unpredictability of life easily leads to feelings of helplessness.

2. **As a result of risk taking:** This includes those who work and serve (soldiers, police officers, paramedics, doctors, detectives, firefighters, and others), who experience horrors that can never be forgotten. No matter how prepared they might have been, and whether they were physically injured or not, the trauma is real. Many in these professions, wanting to look strong, are reluctant to identify problems or ask for help, though they feel helpless and alone.

3. **Self-inflicted:** There is little compassion when you are responsible for your own trauma. In fact, you may receive just the opposite. Felons, drug addicts, drunk drivers, thieves, adulterers, divorced people, and many others have to go on living with anger, resentment, condemnation, persecution, and attacks from others. Misery is magnified through the abandonment by friends, financial losses, and estrangement from family.

Perhaps the origins of your bad choices began long ago through a series of terrible childhood experiences. But the past is no matter now. It may be an explanation, but it is not an excuse.

In many cases we turn our trauma experience against ourselves. Blame, guilt, and shame grow. Serving as our own prosecutor, judge, jury, and warden, we relentlessly punish ourselves with a life sentence without mercy.

Whether you are an innocent victim or caused your own downfall, you deserve a chance to change, to grow, to repent, to be forgiven, to recover and to live a renewed life. It may be difficult, but it can be done.

All of this takes work. Be patient and committed. Healing is not passive. When Bartimaeus wanted Jesus to cure his blindness (Mark 10:46-52), it did not just happen. Jesus asked him, "What do you want me to do for you?" Bartimaeus literally had to take steps toward Jesus. Bartimaeus had to commit and to act. When Christ cures, we all must take our own steps toward healing.

You can. You will. You must. And this book will tell you how.

PART ONE
Trauma Is Everywhere

Obstacles are opportunities, depending on your perspective. That is because the outcome really depends on your decision going into it. This is your life, your survival, and your future.

PART ONE shows the reach of trauma and its effects on virtually everyone. You may have experienced more or less trauma than those around you, but what matters is the impact on you. You can walk free. You can be whole.

Chapter 1

You Are Not Owned by Trauma

In April 1912, the ocean liner *Titanic* sank in the northern At-
lantic Ocean. Over 1,500 people lost their lives. Of the 711
survivors, we know eight more died of suicide (a rate several
times higher than the rest of the population), there were numerous divorces, many refused to ever speak about it, several
died early deaths, and some were institutionalized in mental
asylums.[1] But there were other survivors who did not have these
reactions.

Natural disasters, wars, assaults, abuse, accidents, divorce and
other forms of trauma affect everyone differently.

Trauma leaves some people deeply troubled, some achieve a
functional level of recovery, and some are transformed to new levels of strength.

Those who have faced worse than we have and survived are
beacons of hope in our darkened world.

As you walk along your own journey to health and freedom from trauma, here are ten important points to always
remember:

#1—YOU ARE NOT ALONE

No matter what has happened in the past or what struggles still surround you, you are not alone. Friends and family may have abandoned you out of judgment or condemnation, but others will arise who truly do want to help. You may be tempted to think, "I don't need anyone" or "I'm not worthy of letting others help me," but that is not the case. Embrace humility and let others in. And above all else, remember that God will never abandon you. "Don't be afraid, for I am with you!" (Isaiah 41:10).

#2—YOU ARE NOT THE FIRST

You are neither the first, nor will you be the last. "There is nothing new under the sun" (Ecclesiastes 1:9) is especially true when it comes to trauma. There are others who have survived what afflicts you now. Be open. Don't talk yourself out of listening because of a self-limiting belief that no one could ever possibly understand what you are going through. Others do understand.

#3—YOU CAN THRIVE

You can be a victim *because* of your traumas and be crushed forever . . . or you can survive *despite* what happened to you and take care of yourself and your family. Or your trauma can be the catalyst to become a far better version of yourself than you are right now! Embrace the possibility of triumph.

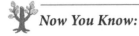 *Now You Know:*

Trauma is not a death sentence and chronic stress is not a life sentence.

#4—YOUR SUFFERINGS DO NOT OWN YOU

Chronic stress is not healthy, but you are a double victim if you convince yourself that stress is in control. Stress does not own you. PTSD does not own you. Fear does not own you. You are not your diagnosis! Your challenges are opportunities to overcome.

#5—YOU HAVE POWER OVER YOUR PAST

Do not let your past determine how you feel about yourself. Memories can be distorted, amplified, diminished, or even forgotten, so don't give your past any control over your present. You are in control of how you think, feel, and act. Leave the past in the past.

#6—KEEP YOUR BRAIN IN CHECK

Your brain controls your emotions, thoughts, and actions. Most of the time, it is your ally, but sometimes it works against you. Stress affects your brain, which then hurts your body. You will heal more quickly when you keep your brain in check.

#7—BE RESILIENT

Resilience is the foundation of inner strength. The experiences of today, both successes and failures, can teach you something. Let your resilience muscles grow as a result of your experiences.

#8—FIGHT BACK WITH RESISTANCE

Your courage, endurance, patience, vigilance, and tenacity can increase to far more than they are right now. That is always the case, for all of us, but it's important to remember. Fight back. Resist!

#9—YOU CAN RECOVER

Recovery from trauma can be very, very difficult, but it is not impossible. It is never impossible. Be open to the possibility of success instead of dwelling on the anxieties of the past. There is an endless supply of hope waiting to be released into your life.

#10—BE RENEWED

You are not in a permanent state of "recovery." Being cognizant of your vulnerabilities does not mean you are weak. In fact, you can go farther than recovery. You can use your trauma to transform into a stronger, smarter, better you!

If you have experienced trauma, always remember that trauma does not own you. You are free to walk free.

That is why you are here!

Chapter 2

Trauma Does Leave a Mark

Paul was an early Apostle, evangelist, and author of much of the Christian Bible's New Testament. Learning about his life will leave you wondering why he was not crippled by depression and PTSD.

Traditionally he is called "Saul" (Hebrew) before his conversion, and "Paul" (Roman) afterwards. As Saul, he was well known for his skills at hunting, arresting, torturing, and throwing people into prison. He was a big deal. The enforcer. The tough guy known for quashing blasphemous believers.

Both feared and revered, Saul had intense convictions. He believed wholeheartedly that he was morally correct in his persecution of early Christians, the new followers of Jesus Christ who had recently been killed by the Romans. Saul knew the scripture warnings if this blasphemy went unchecked, and he would not back down. His job was to convert or rid the world of these blasphemers.

I wonder: Did he ever have any second thoughts? How many trials against Christians did he attend? What did he say in testimony against them? How did he react when they pled for mercy? How did he feel when the accused forgave him in the midst of their torture? How many times did he witness beatings, stoning, arrests, imprisonments, executions? How did those experiences shape his mind and behavior?

One day, while carrying letters of authority to take certain followers of Jesus back to Jerusalem to stand trial, something happened that turned everything he believed upside down. In the Book of Acts, we read:

> He was approaching Damascus, and suddenly a light from heaven flashed around him; and he fell to the ground and heard a voice saying "Saul, Saul, why do you persecute me?" And he said "Who are you, Lord?" and He said "I am Jesus whom you are persecuting, get up and enter the city, and it will be told to you what you must do." The men who were traveling with him stood speechless, hearing the voice but seeing no one. Saul got up from the ground, and though his eyes were open he could see nothing, and leading him by the hand, they brought him into Damascus. And he was three days without sight and neither ate nor drank (Acts 9:3–9; NIV).

Some interpret this as Paul being struck by lightning. Now, lightning is a 200-million volt electrical charge traveling at one-third of the speed of light, which heats the nearby air to 50,000 degrees.

The effects of lightning strikes include mild to severe burns, neurological complications, organ damage, cardiovascular changes (including cardiac arrest), scarring, persistent excruciating pain, and death.[1] Lightning strikes can also be associated with an immediate loss of consciousness, amnesia, confusion, long-term brain injury, sleep disorders, and chronic pain.[2]

 Now You Know:

You did not get to choose what happened to you, but you do get to choose your outcome.

A lightning strike is a serious traumatic event that for many victims results in post-traumatic stress. We do not know if he was actually struck by lightening, but we know at the very least that he was blinded for three days. Sudden blindness is also a severe traumatic event.

I also wonder: What were those three days like? Was he in pain? And once he realized what was really happening to him, was he overcome with guilt over his past behavior? Did he despair? Did he worry that those he had persecuted would turn on him and kill him? Or did he feel a sense of awe and wonder about what had happened and what was to come?

After three days of not eating or drinking, Paul was intently looking for answers when a stranger named Ananias showed up at his door, saying that God had spoken to him in a dream and told him to find Paul and take care of him.

Trusting Ananias with his life, Paul agreed. Then Ananias laid his hands on Paul, and Paul's sight returned.

And immediately there fell from his eyes something like scales, and he regained his sight and got up and was baptized (Acts 9:18).

Baptism is the declared commitment to being a Christian, and Paul had just joined the very group he was trying to destroy.

Talk about a transformational moment, a complete 180-degree turn from everything he believed to be true!

We all experience impactful life events (such as marriage, a new job, retiring, or moving to a new town) that require us to make adaptive changes. But even under those circumstances, we still maintain our core principles and beliefs, friends and family, and outlooks and dreams.

Not so with Paul. Everything changed in those few days. Little did he know that his life would be a nonstop series of even more change, persecution, danger, deprivation, and pain.

Yet through it all, Paul walked free. Somehow, he experienced the severest of traumas, yet he overcame every time. What's more, he ended up being stronger because of it.

By following his example, we can do the same.

SOMEONE WORTH LISTENING TO

When someone has lived and overcome the very worst that life can give, they command your attention. They are worth listening to. Why? Because they possess the unstoppable will and determination to press through and accomplish the impossible.

Quite simply, we respect them because they have been to hell and back. They prove to the world that "no" is not the answer, and in so doing they challenge every one of us to dig deeper, to reach higher, and to press through with our own issues in life.

Paul already had a pretty impressive resumé:

- Multilingual scholar, public speaker, master debater
- Skilled job of a tentmaker
- Bold, loyal, fearless leader
- Able to memorize large amounts of scripture
- Caring, articulate, voracious writer
- Self-sufficient businessman who never asked for anything he did not earn
- Always the victor, never the victim

This is all great, but it's his real-life experiences with trauma that make him worth listening to. Here is a snapshot of what Paul's life looked like after that day on the road to Damascus everything changed:

- Deserted by all his friends
- Escaped from death threats
- Stoned, dragged out of town, and left for dead

- Strong enough to walk thousands of miles
- Able to survive an assassination plot by 40 men
- Five times was whipped 39 lashes
- Stripped naked and left in the cold
- Repeatedly escaping bandits
- Shipwrecked three times
- Lost in the open sea for a day and a night
- Beaten publicly with rods three times
- Bitten by a poisonous viper, which he shook off into the fire
- Repeatedly questioned, threatened, and chased out of towns
- Often deprived of food, water, and sleep
- Falsely arrested many times
- Imprisoned without fair trials
- Chained to a prison wall for two years
- Isolated in Roman jails
- Condemned to death

I've never met someone who has been through even half of these things. But if such a person were alive today, we would want to listen.

That's why people who have overcome seemingly insurmountable odds in life—sports, war, or business—are worth listening to. They have something to say!

PAUL BECAME THE HUNTED

As part of the vilified group, Paul feared for his life. And with good reason: he knew exactly how the persecutors would act because Paul previously hunted those who claimed Jesus was the Messiah as blasphemers of their faith. He changed from hunter to hunted.

From then on, Paul lived with multiple hits on his head. Preaching that Jesus was the Messiah or the Christ was not taken lightly. Many plotted to "do away with him" (Acts 9:23). The gates of the city were watched, but Paul made a harrowing getaway when during the night his disciples lowered him in a basket out a window of the city walls (Acts 9:25).

Paul escaped in the night. For the rest of his life, he would either be relentlessly chased or imprisoned. The traumatic threats never ended.

WHERE ARE THE SIGNS OF TRAUMA?

As much as it would be fascinating to hear Paul speak, I could not help but wonder what he was like when he was "off stage." I mean, who can go through this much pain, loss, torture, near death, rage, disappointment, and unfair treatment . . . and still cope, let alone function in a healthy manner?

I have seen far too many people with traumatic pasts naively assume that Paul would not be a cynical, jealous, angry, weak, hateful individual, with full-blown PTSD symptoms to top it off.

But that's what's strange. Somehow, Paul walked free of it all.

By rights, he should at least have been overcome by what we call Complex Post Traumatic Stress Disorder. C-PTSD is a psychological disorder stemming from protracted and extreme psychological and physical cruelty. You see it in children who grow up in abusive homes; people who have suffered from long-term intimate partner violence; those held in captivity due to kidnapping or slavery; holocaust survivors; prisoners of war; and victims of abusive cults.

Understandably, victims of C-PTSD have considerable difficulty developing social relationships and trust, and regulating their own emotions long after they are free of the abuse. They usually experience "dissociative" symptoms, where they feel disconnected from the world around them. They may even have amnesia surrounding the traumatic events, depersonalization (feeling separated from their own thoughts or body), derealization (a sense that the world is distorted and unreal), or even lose sense of their identity or personality.

Yet, some people are able to let go of the emotional baggage normally associated with such trauma. What's their secret to being free?

 Now You Know:

You have the ability to come out of this in a way that makes you even better than you were before.

How did Paul walk free?

Was it his character? His attitude? His belief system? Sheer will and determination? Some secret power? Gratitude?

We know he wasn't immune to despair because he wrote:

> We were under great pressure, far beyond our ability to endure, so that we despaired of life itself. Indeed, we felt we had received the sentence of death (2 Corinthians 1:8–9, NIV).

Even then, he did not give up. He could have, but he didn't.

But would you really blame him if he suffered flashbacks, nightmares, anxiety attacks, insomnia, eating disorders, chronic illness, debilitating pain, cognitive decline, amnesia, early dementia, inability to work, physical disabilities, alcoholism, addiction, isolation, loneliness, personality disorders, delusions, depression, or suicide?

These are common. I see the stats every day.

PAUL LEFT HIS RELIGION

Leaving a religion can itself be a traumatic event. Paul's new beliefs as a Christian (the Messiah, tried and crucified on a cross as a criminal, who rose from the dead) conflicted with his former beliefs as a Pharisee.

Major change in core religious beliefs can be accompanied by considerable emotional distress. Called Religious Trauma Syndrome, this comes from severing ties with a religion, particularly if the former was authoritarian.

Paul's old religion had a clear worldview that gave meaning and purpose to his life through teaching, ritual, and religious practice, all reinforced by violent actions toward anyone whose beliefs or behaviors undermined the established religious practices.

The emotional, physical, and spiritual impact of leaving a religion can be enormous, but it did not break Paul.

Paul could have been the one curled up in a fetal position night after night, waking up in a drenching sweat, but he wasn't.

The continuously best-selling book of all time, the Bible—Paul helped write a good portion of it. And some of the most famous words about love were written by him, including:

Love is patient, love is kind. It does not envy, it does not boast, it is not proud. It does not dishonor others, it is not self-seeking, it is not easily angered, it keeps no record of wrongs. Love does not delight in evil but rejoices with the truth. It always protects, always trusts, always hopes, always perseveres (1 Corinthians 13:4–6 NIV).

These are profound words written by a man who understandably could have taken an opposite approach. How could the same guy who suffered so much be grounded in love?

Instead of breaking down mentally, his strength grew with every trial he faced, eventually becoming one of the most influential persons in the history of civilization.

How did all this happen?

After decades of working with people, counseling, training, helping, and searching for answers, I have come to believe that Paul's secret to staying healthy was a combination of four connected yet foundational ingredients.

It looks like this:

1. Paul's psychological and spiritual **Resilience**
2. gave him the armor for his **Resistance,**
3. which gave him hope for his **Recovery,**
4. where his **Renewal** completely changed his life through his faith.

Are you battling trauma? Who isn't? In truth, we all have our own impossible challenges to overcome.

The good news is that what worked for Paul will also work for us.

So, regardless of what you have gone through, regardless of your trauma, regardless of what people or circumstances may say, there is hope. There are answers. You can break away from your pain and find true joy in a newer, more meaningful life.

You can get healthy.

Trauma leaves a mark—so let it be a sign of your greater strength, bolder love, deeper passion, and stronger grip on this life you get to live!

Chapter 3

How Trauma Affects You

Years ago, I was in a rollover accident in Iraq. We were driving to the Bagdad Airport at night when our vehicle was forced off the road and over a concrete barrier.

As we rolled, I was tossed around like a piece of popcorn in a pot. My head slammed against the armored steel interior, leaving me with cuts around my eye, a neck injury, temporary paralysis of my arms, and a concussion.

With my brain in a fog, I could hardly think. I was strapped to a backboard, my neck was immobilized with a brace, and I was whisked away for medical help. My hands were shaking uncontrollably.

The corpsman explained in a very matter-of-fact voice, "It's just your adrenaline."

TRAUMA EFFECTS ON YOUR BRAIN AND BODY

Trauma affects every part of you, from head to toe. That's because your brain and your hormones are directly affected by trauma, and those in turn affect every cubic inch of your body.

That is one reason trauma is so complicated, because it is neither fully physical and nor fully mental. It is a combination of both, and that requires extra effort and extra patience.

Most of us, however, are impatient with ourselves. But if you broke your leg, would you expect to be able to walk on it tomorrow? Of course not, and our brain is incredibly complicated, yet we are so impatient with the slow speed of recovery from trauma.

Honestly, will anxiety, memories, and stress magically disappear overnight? No.

It is important that you give yourself permission to take time to heal, and that applies to the results of trauma across the board.

When our brain is working properly, we take in information through our senses, connect it to past learning, do a quick analysis, review possible responses, and choose appropriate action. All this comes in pretty handy when facing our day-to-day decisions.

But if trauma is sustained over a long period of time, our brain cells and their interconnections undergo physical changes. Our body and brain remain in a constant state of protective high alert, and the longer this goes on, the harder it is to calm the system down. As a direct result, our body's organs are damaged and become less efficient and more prone to disease.

Trauma really does affect you, both mentally and physically. The fact is, every part of the brain is affected by trauma. The brain's job is to protect us from real threats. When trauma trains the brain to *always* expect the worst, real or imagined, which causes very real changes in the architecture of the brain and can lead to serious problems: Consider the following:

1. **Ever have memories that are distorted, behaviors that are inappropriate, or judgment that is flawed?** That's the frontal cortex being affected by trauma.
2. **Ever confuse routine activities, become increasingly forgetful, or keep getting lost on the way home?** That's the hippocampus being affected by trauma.

3. **Ever struggle with exaggerated emotional responses to pain, have trouble stopping an addiction?** That's the insular cortex being affected by trauma.

4. **Ever want to impulsively retaliate in anger—but you know better—and then you do it anyway?** That's the anterior cingulate cortex being affected by trauma.

5. **Ever have trouble regulating stress hormones, maintaining body temperature, being hungry when you shouldn't be, having trouble sleeping, or feeling extra fearful?** That's the hypothalamus being affected by trauma.

6. **Ever have feelings of intense fear as if there is a clear and present danger even though it is only a past memory of something that no longer exists or a worry about something that has never happened?** That's the amygdala affected by trauma. By the way, the accumulation of these fear responses actually causes the amygdala to grow bigger, which further exaggerates our fear response.

Some are quick to say, "It's all in your head," but that's not 100 percent true, though it sure makes you pause and consider when you realize just how much the brain affects your body's physical performance.

It's always both, mental and physical, that are affected by trauma, and being aware of that reality will help you in many ways.

TRAUMA EFFECTS ON YOUR HORMONES

Just as trauma affects your brain, so it affects your hormones. And hormones, as you well know, affect every part of your body, even down at the cellular level.

1. **Adrenaline and trauma:** When your fight or flight response is triggered, there is an immediate release of adrenaline

(norepinephrine) into your body. This suppresses your appetite, slows digestion, and directs your energy toward dealing with the danger you face. At the same time, you may sweat, your hands may shake, and your heart may race.

Eventually, you do calm down, but what's interesting about adrenaline and your body is that later, even weeks or months later, when you mentally replay the incident, the same physical symptoms can return. No wonder remembering feels so very real!

 Now You Know:

Physical and psychological stress, major depression, and PTSD shrink your brain's volume, but a healthy diet, relaxation, and sleep will help heal your brain.

2. **Cortisol and trauma:** In a fight or flight scenario, cortisol is released into your body to help you prepare against threats and respond if you are injured. Long-term release of cortisol, however, can cause depression, cardiovascular disease, diabetes, weight gain, and weakens your immune system.[1] It actually destroys your brain.

   Holocaust survivors have been found to still have abnormally low cortisol levels, which illustrates the long-term impact of severe childhood trauma.[2] A different study found adolescent refugees from war-torn Syria had both abnormally high and low levels of cortisol in the children.[3]

   And whether the stress is real or imagined, your body still produces cortisol. Prolonged exposure to cortisol is what you must avoid.

3. **Cytokines and trauma:** The cytokines hormones are a benefit to you. They increase or decrease inflammation as needed, help your immune system, support nerve cell function, and keep your body's reaction to stress under control.

However, when stress levels stay up, the inflammation from cytokines cause damage. That includes heart disease, increased risk for a heart attack, autoimmune disease, periodontal disease, delayed wound healing, neurodegeneration, sleep disorders, a weakened immune system, more allergic reactions and asthma, memory loss, and depression.[4,5,6] As if that's not enough, prolonged exposure increases your risk for PTSD,[7] and if cytokine levels remain too high, arthritis, cancer, influenza, and death may result.

WHY DO WE "BURN OUT"?

We have to live with stress to a certain degree, as it is a natural part of life, but we do not want to burn out from too much for too long.

You don't even have to face life-threatening situations to get your brain and hormones working against you. Persistent stress from work demands, daily commutes, being around difficult/toxic people, and a dysfunctional family counts as major stress.

Even counselors who work with trauma victims end up being affected themselves.

The fact is, we burn out because we were just not made to carry stress and trauma forever. Our bodies are amazingly adaptive, but there is a breaking point that we cannot mentally, physically, emotionally, or spiritually endure. We can try to delay the burnout by self-medicating with alcohol, drugs, and vices. But we will not escape the impact of stress if we do not change the cause.

For me, I unfortunately learned at a young age to connect my self-esteem to my work ethic. The harder I worked and the more productive I was, the better I felt about myself. It drove me through high school, college, grad school, faculty positions, writing for journals, being on TV and radio, and a run for State

Senate. I helped enact a major law dealing with health-care reform, coauthored *The Angry Child*, ran for US Congress, raised millions in campaign funds, authored *Overcoming Passive Aggression*, and passed the most significant mental health reform bill in the past 50 years.

If that wasn't enough, I enlisted as an officer in the US Navy Medical Service Corps as a psychologist treating traumatic brain injury and post-traumatic stress (including regular work at Walter Reed National Military Medical Center at Bethesda, with active-duty training aboard three aircraft carriers and with Navy Special Warfare).

But linking self-worth (who I am) with hard work and productivity (what I do) is admittedly a recipe for disaster. I paid no attention to the toll it was taking on me, my family, or my marriage; to the lingering problems of growing up in a home with a sometimes-violent alcoholic father; or to my own battles with depression.

I lived tired, on edge, hypercritical of myself and others, and always unhappy on the inside. I was burned out. I was winning the whole world and losing my soul (Matthew 16:26).

My cure? To work even harder! And eventually, I burned all the way out.

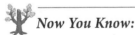 *Now You Know:*

If you are not improving as quickly as you want to, it is not because you are a bad person, abandoned, forgotten, or being punished. The traumatized brain simply takes time to heal.

The breakthrough for me was when I let go and pulled the plug on all the misdirected hard work and productivity, and focused instead on saving my family. It was hard for me to do what I needed to do, but had I not done that, I would have lost everything.

Whatever your level of trauma and stress, recognize that it's having a negative impact on your body. Take action now before you do burn out.

WHAT ARE PTS AND PTSD?

Trauma and stress can result in a wide range of temporary or chronic psychological symptoms. Post-traumatic stress (PTS) is the short-term impact of trauma that affects your sleep, work, concentration, and social relationships.

When the symptoms last longer and are more debilitating, PTS escalates to Post Traumatic Stress Disorder (PTSD). Here are several PTSD symptoms:

- Recurrent, unrelenting, and intrusive memories of the traumatic event (including flashbacks and nightmares triggering severe emotional distress);
- Avoidance (not thinking or talking about the trauma);
- Profound changes in thinking/mood marked by difficulties maintaining close relationships;
- Emotional numbing;
- Changes in emotions that lead to sleep disorders, trouble concentrating, self-destructive behavior, anger, and overwhelming guilt or shame.

PTSD can have a lasting medical impact, such as the increase in heart disease among first responders to the 9/11 World Trade Center attack[8] and veterans.[9]

PTSD can happen to anyone. Among the military, between 10 percent and 20 percent of those who served in combat develop PTSD symptoms sometime after their deployment. Although the majority of combat service members do not develop the full symptoms of PTSD, most will experience a level of temporary combat stress, known simply as Post Traumatic Stress or PTS as a normal and expected reaction to the severe conditions of warfare.

Even veterans who were not in direct combat (such as air combat drone operators who attack the enemy while looking at their video screen, or those who witness training accidents) can still develop PTSD.

Since only 1 percent of the US population serves in the military, most people who develop PTS or PTSD are nonmilitary. Hospital emergency department nurses, police, firefighters, and EMS professionals are 10 times more likely than the general population to develop PTSD.

However, anyone is at risk who has been the victim of or an eyewitness to a life-threatening or harmful event, such as an auto accident, kidnapping, fire, flood, shooting, or fight. It can also result from intense emotional trauma, such as a broken close relationship, betrayal, divorce, personal financial devastation, or abuse as a child or adult.

A diagnosis of PTSD requires that you be directly or indirectly impacted by a traumatic event. Seeing a scary movie or reading a frightening story is not a traumatic event. It may be very upsetting, but it's not PTSD.

It is worth noting that if you have lived with prolonged intense stress, such as relentlessly troubling family relationships, chronic illness, severe financial strains, unemployment, or a disability, then the cumulative impact can be just as harmful to your body and brain as a single traumatic event. The effects of prolonged stress may not be classified as PTSD, but the impact of chronic high stress levels can still be severe.

Most people will eventually return to normal by talking with supportive family and friends, taking time off to heal, getting plenty of rest, and focusing on the goal of getting better.

For others, however, the harm runs deeper. They are not "returning to normal," and they wonder if something is wrong with them.

If that's you, and you are taking longer to get better, let me say this:

"Slow does not mean never. You will get better."

Hurt happens, but healing happens too.

Keep working at it. You have a great deal of strength within you, even if you do not believe it yet. History is full of examples of ordinary people who encountered extraordinary hardships but achieved incredible success. You can do the same!

The degree of our PTS reaction is affected not just by the severity of the event but also by our resilience. I have known people overwhelmed by minor afflictions while other people who were unscathed or even strengthened by a far more severe calamity.

Watching people experience affliction and then recover has taught me that the event itself is not necessarily destructive. The outcome depends on how we handle adversity and interpret it, and the tools we use for recovery.

Thankfully, pain is never forever. So why not let this be your stepping stone to health and freedom!

PAUL WAS SHUNNED

Religious changes, betrayal, and broken assumptions can be traumatic. They have been found to lead directly to the doubt, fear, and vulnerability that is often experienced by those with PTSD.

Paul was shunned by his former Jewish circles while simultaneously facing suspicion as he joined the followers of Jesus. The stress of being despised by the group you left and mistrusted by the group you are joining has to be considerable.

In many respects, he became a refugee. That is fertile ground for mental disorders, yet Paul stood strong.

PAUL KNEW HOW TO HANDLE STRESS

Honestly, I am astonished that Paul did not succumb to total burnout from long travels, hunger, imprisonment, abandonment, robbery, sleep deprivation, and torture. All of this surely must have taken a brutal toll on his brain, hormones, and body.

But instead of collapsing or centering all his attention on himself, Paul remained dedicated to his mission. He remained steadfast throughout. He was in it to win it. He wrote: "Do you not know that in a race all the runners run, but only one receives the prize? So run that you may obtain it" (1 Corinthians 9:24 ESV).

 Now You Know:

Trauma is not meant to be denied, ignored, or covered up. It's meant to be addressed, dealt with, and used as a foundation for growth.

Paul's traumas never ended, so you think that eventually he would have perpetual mental fog, problems with verbal memory, and be emotionally blunted. Yet, he wrote prolifically, taught daily, traveled constantly, and loved dearly.

Paul is an incredible example of how this amazing creation of our brain can withstand and rebuild despite protracted and intense psychological trauma. Paul took control of his life, and did not focus on his pain. Instead, he saw his own pain as important for his own healing. There may have been guilt for past mistakes, but he didn't view himself as a failure.

Your brain is the central control for your reactions to threats and stress, whether actual or psychological. We will discuss specific methods of healing later in the book, but for now, know this:

> While stress and trauma can harm your brain and body, your brain can heal, and your body will follow suit.

Which means it is possible! There is always hope, and you can succeed as well.

PART TWO
Steps to Healing

The four foundational steps for your healing from trauma

Step #1—Build Your Own Resilience

Step #2—Arm Your Resistance

Step #3—Embrace Your Recovery

Step #4—Accept Your Renewal

Chapter 4

Step #1—Build Your Own Resilience

When I worked at Children's Hospital of Pittsburgh, I got to know many families of children inflicted with life-threatening diseases. I have particularly fond memories of Jordan and his family. Their resilience was awe inspiring.

I had moved on to another job and had not seen them for a few years, but ran into the parents one day at a store.

"How is Jordan?" I asked, as soon as I got close enough to talk.

They told me Jordan had died a few months earlier.

I started to choke up and could only say, "I am so sorry."

"Please don't feel bad," the mother replied.

She smiled sweetly and then said some of the most profound words I have ever heard someone say, "All of this was the best thing that ever could have happened to us. He made us into a family. We are closer than ever and continue to be close. All because of him."

That is resilience! It was within them all along, and it shines brightly, even to this day. They recognize that resilience and celebrate it.

 Scripture Says:

Prepare your work outside; get everything ready for yourself in the field, and after that build your house (Proverbs 24:27 ESV).

RESILIENCE IS WITHIN YOU

Resilience prepares us for what lies ahead. It gives us the strength to endure. It enables us to press on, to fight forward, and effectively manage our stress.

Like the phrase I often hear from Marines, "What doesn't kill me makes me stronger," resilience gets stronger and stronger over time. But it will not happen passively. We all need to work at it.

You have probably seen (or even have it as a tattoo) the popular verse:

I can do all things through Christ who strengthens me (Philippians 4:13 NKJV).

Did you know that Paul wrote those words while in a Roman prison awaiting execution? That sure gives a little more meaning and perspective to his words! Imprisoned, yes, but not conquered by any means.

Here are the five choices that make up your resilience:

1. Choose strength (over weakness).
2. Choose discipline (over disorganization).
3. Choose solitude (over isolation).
4. Choose humility (over pride).
5. Choose goals (over chaos).

RESILIENCE IN YOUR STRENGTH

Strength is a choice in action, requiring a decision and a steadfast commitment to build on it, step by step.

And life as we know it will be tough, just as Scripture plainly states:

> In this world you will have trouble (John 15:33 NIV).

Be prepared for it by responding with strength.

Some people refuse to move forward, choosing weakness. Don't give in to weakness, even for a moment, because that trail leads to fear, avoidance, insecurity, and broken dreams.

Paul learned much about building strength when he lived in Corinth, a city on the isthmus connecting mainland Greece and the Peloponnese peninsula. Corinth was a cosmopolitan city where goods were transported over this land shortcut. Entire ships were unloaded on one side, moved across the four-mile isthmus, and then reloaded onto another ship. It took less time and far less risk than sailing 200 miles around the peninsula through treacherous waters.

Travelers would seek local entertainment as they waited to get their goods moved. A major attraction was the "Isthmian games," which were held every two years, drawing athletes and big crowds. Paul's skills as a tentmaker were in demand for travelers needing tent repairs as they passed through Corinth. This gave Paul a "front row seat" to watch the athletes train for these games.

The Isthmian games included boxing, foot races, wrestling, and pankration (similar to today's cage fighting). In these contests there were no bronze or silver medals. You won or you lost.

Paul observed the strategies of champions: to win you had to work hard, be strong, and prepare. He wrote:

> So I do not run aimlessly, nor do I box as though beating
> the air (1 Corinthian 9:26 NRSV).

In strength, with training and dedication, you prepare to win.

RESILIENCE IN YOUR DISCIPLINE

Strength is good and necessary, but discipline controls strength and gives it a purpose for good. Discipline is all about self-control of the body, mind, words, and emotions aimed toward being better and improving. It is an attitude of constant improvement and intolerance for mediocrity.

Natural ability without discipline tends to drift into mediocrity.

Discipline is not a spectator sport. No matter how much talent people have, the prize goes to the one who stays on task until it is completed. That is discipline.

Paul understood that, for he penned these words:

> I discipline my body and make it my slave, so that, after I have preached to others, I myself will not be disqualified (1 Corinthians 9:27 NASB).

Discipline is constant effort, even if the steps are small. At least they are going in the right direction, and that builds your strength mentally, physically, emotionally, and spiritually.

Being disciplined means you do not demand a soft and protected life. You don't give the responsibility or control of your life to others. It is always your own responsibility, not theirs.

 Now You Know:

When it comes down to it, resilience comes from within. It is personal. It is yours.

You are responsible for you, which means you prepare yourself for any future challenges that might await you.

That is the best preparation for the best future possible.

Stay disciplined, keep moving forward, for that builds your confidence little by little to push through pain, frustration, doubt, boredom, and fear.

RESILIENCE IN YOUR SOLITUDE

Solitude is an intentional, self-controlled quiet, where you process your thoughts, feelings, and actions with depth and honesty. The attitude of solitude is that of emotional comfort to yourself, calming behaviors that nurture health, and thoughts that build self-awareness and confidence.

It is during these quiet times alone that you do your most constructive work within your own mind, heart, spirit, and action. It allows us to focus on what is important now, and not get distracted by anxious clutter.

Solitude is not the same as quiet "serenity," where you only think peaceful, relaxing thoughts. Not at all. Solitude is a time to work on yourself and clarify your thoughts, so that you can move forward.

 Now You Know:

Solitude is your opportunity to build resilience, but isolation undermines your resilience.

Solitude is also not "isolation," which is more about hiding, trying not to think, and distracting yourself from dealing with real issues. There is tremendous temptation to escape the pain of trauma by isolating ourselves from the world. It's one of the symptoms of PTSD. Isolation leads you down a trail of incompleteness, and can trigger depression and anxiety.

In true solitude, you can sit alone, totally comfortable with the company you keep. There is a calm confidence that you are making progress on yourself. That prevents feelings of loneliness or desperation.

This intentional openness to quietly listen empowers you to deal directly with issues as they arise. In this safe place, you are comfortable with your own discomfort.

Perhaps this is where you quietly grieve the death of a friend, experience the sadness of disappointment, have honest conversations with yourself, or deepen your understanding of your life. Genuine emotions are welcomed, not avoided.

As a result, solitude actually helps you become closer to others, because as you take the time to better understand yourself, you will not appear desperate or confused when talking with others. Solitude clears your head so you can truly listen to others without any mental distractions or neediness.

In addition, solitude is the place for creative thought. Nikola Tesla, one of the most brilliant inventors of all time, said it well, "Originality thrives in seclusion free of outside influences beating upon us to cripple the creative mind. Be alone, that is the secret of invention; be alone, that is when ideas are born."[1]

In solitude, you set aside all distractions, turn off all media, and say out loud, "I'm listening, God. Talk to me." Then you shut up and listen. There are no more important voices than God's and your own. Listen and learn. "Be still and know that I am God" (Psalm 46:10 NABRE).

RESILIENCE IN YOUR HUMILITY

I once asked a Navy SEAL commander what the number one personality trait was that he sought in team members. Without hesitation, he responded, "Humility."

The attitude of humility involves honesty, a drive to learn, respect, willingness to sacrifice, and gratitude. An arrogant person, however, is boastful, blames others, can't learn from their own mistakes, takes credit for unearned success, is dishonest, wallows in self-pity over failures, and undermines the success of others.

Who would you want beside you in battle?

Resilience grows with humility. Always, when it comes to dealing with issues, honesty is the best policy. It takes a lot of humility to be honest about where you are strong and where you may need more work.

Humility is the way we grow, mature, and achieve what we are chasing after.

Taking steps toward the freedom and life you want requires all the aspects of humility. It also requires an honest assessment of your abilities, not overconfident or underconfident. Just be honest. No more. No less.

When you are honest with yourself, there is no room to put yourself down, or to claim you are too weak to heal or change.

I often hear people say such things, but that is not honesty at all. It's a lie that is based on the belief that they are the only person in the history of humankind totally incapable of ever getting better or that their mistake was proof that they will always be a failure.

That is not just illogical, it's impossible! Humility accepts failure and pain, learns from them, and moves on. Nothing can hold you down and nothing is permanent. Let it go.

And if you do need help, ask for it and do whatever is required.

That's humility in action. Each time you practice humility, it builds your confidence and strengthens your resilience.

Paul knew well the Bible story of Job, a man who lost all his wealth and family. Job wanted to challenge God to ask him why he had to endure so much suffering. Think of the response he received as the way a loving parent would answer an ungrateful teen who claims, "You never do anything for me." Job was told to get ready for what he was about to hear: "Brace yourself like a man." Because he was going to get a series of questions that would knock the hubris out of him. Here are a few of the questions asked of Job

> Where were you when I laid the foundations of the earth?
> Tell Me if you have understanding . . .
> Have you ever in your life commanded the morning,

And caused the dawn to know its place?
Have you entered into the springs of the sea
Or walked in the recesses of the deep?
Have the gates of death been revealed to you,
Or have you seen the gates of deep darkness?
Have you understood the expanse of the earth?
Tell *Me*, if you know all this . . .
Where is the way that the light is divided,
Or the east wind scattered on the earth? (Job 38 NASB)

This is not a sarcastic celestial smackdown. Rather, this was a grand-scale lesson on humility taught with wisdom, respect, and real love. We rarely understand the struggles of the present, but if we approach with humility, we will be better equipped to understand when our troubles are in the past.

RESILIENCE IN YOUR GOALS

You are going somewhere, and that forward movement is the result of your goals, whatever your goals might be. It looks something like this:

- **Goals** determine where you want to go.
- **Plans** keep you on track with well-defined and achievable steps toward your goals.
- **Strategies** are the flexible, adaptable actions you take to achieve your plans, making changes as needed.

You have no doubt heard that goals without plans are just dreams. That's true, but plans without strategies run the risk of getting stuck when situations change.

Quite simply, you need:

goals + plans + strategies

Now You Know:

If you have no clearly defined destination, anything looks like action. When you have all three parts working together, you build resilience.

The fact is, you need clear direction in life to be and do all that is within you. That is true for everyone, and specifically speaking, this also applies to recovering from the traumas of life. Having goals + plans + strategies is a recipe for lifesaving resilience.

When Hurricane Katrina hit the city of New Orleans in 2005, the flooding impacted over 100,000 homes and businesses and more than 1,800 people died. Did you know that the levee system was built to code—code that required it to withstand a category-3 hurricane? Hurricane Katrina was a category-5 storm, and the rest is history.

Finger pointing after the fact does not fix anything. Had they originally set sufficiently high goals, had clear plans, and then applied appropriate construction strategies, the result would have been very different.

The we'll-see-what-happens approach (some call it "luck") is no way to live, and when it comes to trauma, that approach is downright dangerous.

Why? Because trauma victims who do not set goals to get healthy and free end up suffering and in bondage to their trauma.

But the reverse is also true! Every trauma victim I have ever worked with who was committed to a clear set of goals, a plan, and strategies to reach them was far more resilient against long-term debilitating symptoms from trauma.

Goals increase your resilience, and resilience helps pull you through.

※ ※ ※

Recognize the resilience inside of you. Let it shine brighter every single day. It's there. You know it, because it's in your:

- Strength
- Discipline
- Solitude
- Humility
- Goals

Your resilience is powerful.

Chapter 5

How to Apply Your Resilience

Marie has been a police officer for almost 20 years. She has been repeatedly threatened and assaulted, and has investigated countless murder scenes. Her toughest memories to deal with, however, are the children who were starved, hurt, or killed.

"I can't stop seeing what I've seen," she says.

She used to drink heavily but was able to quit. Her first marriage ended in divorce, and her second one was headed in the same direction. The long, unpredictable work hours, combined with her tendency to isolate and say little at home, was destroying her marriage and her relationship with her children.

Instead of letting history repeat itself, she decided to take action. She knew her drinking, her isolation, and her silence at home were not healthy ways to deal with trauma. So she made some changes.

Now when she comes home, she takes 15 minutes of solitude to reorient her mind and heart. She leaves work at work and focuses on family. During that time, she reminds herself with gratitude that she is home, safe, and with her caring husband and children. Then she reconnects with her family and is able to be patient, calm, and caring.

Her trauma is very real, and usually daily, but she has learned how to apply her own resilience so that she can have the life she wants.

That's what she chose.

YOU GET TO CHART YOUR COURSE

All resilience is a choice. Once you have chosen resilience to be part of your life, you are prepared in advance for things that come your way, no matter how big or small they might be.

Preparedness through resilience applies in these common areas:

- in your strength;
- in your discipline;
- in your solitude;
- in your humility;
- in your goals.

You get to choose. My suggestion is that you apply all of them to your life, and keep applying them every step of the way. That's what I do.

It becomes a habit.

HOW TO APPLY STRENGTH

Traumatic events may require your physical, emotional, mental, or spiritual strength to combat and overcome. But as you know, stress takes a toll on your body.

For example, it's been said that first responders describe their day as 90 percent boredom and 10 percent terror. They face all sorts of dangerous situations, and with it the adrenalin rushes, images, and trauma. It takes a toll.

The firefighter often does not get much rest, and when they finally fall asleep, every alarm makes them bolt out of bed, with heart racing as they don their gear and rush to the fire. Interestingly, firefighters (who must also be strong and physically fit) are more likely to die from a heart attack than from smoke inhalation, burns, building collapses, or accidents on the way to a fire.[1]

There are many benefits to building physical strength. The better your physical condition:

- the greater your physical resilience;
- the quicker you are able to recover;
- the more stamina and endurance you have;
- the less likely stress will slow you down.

Your resilience requires that you be physically strong. Don't be intimidated by that fact. Be strong by choosing to build your strength.

Emotional strength is also required. Life's disappointments, hurts, and heartbreaks require emotional strength to deal with them. If not, it's easy to spiral into hopelessness, doubt, worry, and fear.

Yes, life is also filled with times of glorious joy, beauty, and love, but the fun and easy times do not make you strong. It's the hard times, the tough experiences, that build your emotional strength.

Though we may want a stress-free life, we all know that is not going to happen! We also know, or at least admit, that the absence of stress does not build emotional resilience. An easy life actually weakens resilience.

There are many benefits to building emotional strength. The better your emotional condition:

- the greater your emotional resilience;
- the greater your confidence in your decision-making;
- the less likely you are to be depressed, feel anxious, or be self-centered;

- the better you will be at making friends, managing relationships, and solving problems;
- the quicker you recover from trauma.

PAUL KNEW HOW TO STAND FIRM

With full knowledge of the many difficulties we face in this life, Paul advised us to stand firm, to not give up, and to outfit ourselves fully with the Armor of God in our fight against evil.

Paul's description of the soldier outfitted for battle is a great metaphor of the attitudes needed to endure in our own battles:

> Therefore, put on the full armor of God, so that when the day of evil comes, you may be able to stand your ground, and after you have done everything, to stand. Stand firm then, with the belt of truth buckled around your waist, with the breastplate of righteousness in place, and with your feet fitted with the readiness that comes from the gospel of peace. In addition to all this, take up the shield of faith, with which you can extinguish all the flaming arrows of the evil one (Ephesians 6:13-17 NIV).

Paul understood that it was the Lord who equips us with what we need. He wrote:

> It is God who is at work in you, enabling you both to will and to work for his good pleasure (Philippians 2:13 NRSV).

Your resilience is strength to confront your troubles. It is you making the choice to overcome, no matter what it takes.

Paul built his emotional strength by focusing on the payoff, not the pain. He explained it this way:

> For I consider that the sufferings of this present time are not worthy to be compared with the glory that is to be revealed to us (Romans 8:18 NAB).

Your own suffering is far more manageable when you release yourself from the misery of the moment and view your emotional strains as temporary. Even in Paul's final days before his beheading, he wrote a letter to Timothy encouraging him to stay emotionally strong in the face of fear:

> Now let it grow, as a small flame grows into a fire. God did not give us a spirit that makes us afraid. He gave us a spirit of power and love and self-control (2 Timothy 1:6–7 NKJV).

Even after decades of suffering and a looming death sentence, Paul did not give in to emotional weakness. He remained in control rather than letting his emotions control him.

Mental strength is also required. Mental toughness is the ability to maintain a sharp mind, under pressure, with the wisdom to think beyond your experience. A weak mind is susceptible to mistakes and will have a difficult time making rational decisions under even slight pressure.

The best way to build mental toughness is to actively rehearse mental toughness under pressure. In other words, you practice. There are many benefits to building mental strength. The better your mental condition:

- the greater your mental resilience;
- the better your decisions under pressure;
- the stronger you are to overcome limiting situations;
- the less control trauma has on your mind.

Now You Know:

With rare exceptions, great art, music masterpieces, and successes of-
ten come after years (often 10 years or more) of work.

Lastly, *spiritual strength* is also required. Paul warned us 2,000
years ago:

> Be watchful, stand firm in the faith, act like men, be
> strong (1 Corinthians 16:13).

There are many benefits to building spiritual strength. The
better your spiritual condition:

- the greater your spiritual resilience;
- the less likely you are to succumb to temptations;
- the more likely you are to control your own thoughts;
- the stronger your mind, heart, and body will be.

Strength resilience (physical, emotional, mental, and spiritual) is
evident in those who have it. And if you have it, you are on the right
track! If you need more of it, keep working, because it will come.

Here are five strength-building tips to apply if needed:

1. **Commit to getting stronger.** When this is your mindset and
   your attitude, your actions will follow.
2. **Surround yourself with friends who will reinforce at-**
   titudes of strength. Avoid people who pull you down into
   weakness.
3. **Focus on the positives.** Don't whine, play the victim, or share
   your plights openly on social media. That keeps you weak.
4. **Overcome timidity.** Volunteer to help others who are struggling. As you support their growth, you will grow stronger in
   your own resilience.
5. **Track your growth.** Log your progress in a journal. Review
   where you were and where you are, which will give you insight
   into where you are going.

HOW TO APPLY DISCIPLINE

As with strength, discipline comes in several forms. You need discipline to overcome whatever obstacles you face.

 Scripture Says:

Seek these out on your own and read them: Exodus 15:2; Psalm 9:9; Joshua 1:9.

To be strong, you need mental discipline. Without it, stress has a way of overwhelming you, concentrating is difficult, distractions come easily, and even thinking is harder than it should be.

A disciplined mind remains in control. This is vitally important, especially when it comes to "taking every thought captive" (2 Corinthians 10:5 NASB) so you are able to remain focused on what is most important to you.

It is so easy for an undisciplined mind to get sucked into the world of "what ifs?" I've seen small interruptions or accidents send people into a fear-filled frenzy. They completely fall apart. But what is interesting is that other people, who went through the exact same experience at the exact same time, remain in control.

The bottom line is this:

If you control your mind, you control your body.

To build mental discipline so you can remain in control, apply these six steps:

1. Set the mental goal of mastering your challenge.
2. Break it down into its parts.
3. Mentally rehearse each part.
4. Imagine possible difficulties to overcome.
5. Practice positive self-talk of success through each step.

When you mentally practice doing something right, you increase your odds of winning considerably. And the more you practice, the greater your success rate.

Why? Because every time you rehearse, your brain gets stronger. It gets used to winning, achieving, and overcoming. And then you do it. Sure, it will take time, but there is no question that it's worth it.

Mental discipline also helps you overcome fear. The mentally undisciplined are likely to panic because they are not prepared. It's as simple as that.

You probably heard about Alex Honnold, the man who free-climbed (without safety ropes) the "El Capitan" 3,200-foot vertical cliff in Yosemite National Park back in 2017. They actually scanned his brain and found that he was able to control his own brain and turn off his brain's fear center. He also physically practiced with safety ropes for seven years before he was ready!

Just like Paul taught, Alex learned how to make his body a slave to his mind. You can do the same.

 Now You Know:

Run toward opportunities to master discipline. You are going to need those skills anyway.

Mental discipline is not the only form of discipline to work on. There is also:

- **Discipline of your body:** Whatever level you prepare for is the level at which you will deliver. Practice strong, perform strong. A disciplined body not only helps keep you physically healthy, but also helps you handle everyday emotional and mental stress.

    If you want muscles, you work out. If you want stamina, you keep working out. And if you want stamina for stress, then discipline yourself through difficult situations.

Paul was constantly disciplining his body and mind. Without it, how could he have survived the shipwrecks, floating at sea for a day and a half, multiple beatings with canes, a stoning, and five whippings of 39 lashes? It was his mental discipline over the physical exhaustion and pain that helped him survive these traumatic events. You can do the same.

- **Discipline of your words:** You can tell a lot about people by the words they use. Do they use a lot of "me" and "I" and "my," or do they use words like "we" and "us" and "our"? Those who are proud, arrogant, and conceited use words that match.

  While Paul spent his days talking, teaching, and debating with others, he was careful that his words would not appear haughty, lest they distract from his message. And he had a reminder to make sure his words remained humble. He referred to his continuous pain "in order to keep me from becoming conceited, I was given a thorn in my flesh, a messenger of Satan, to torment me" (2 Corinthians 12:7 NIV). We don't know exactly what caused this pain, but we do know it helped him carefully select the right words to teach, comfort, and inspire others. Paul advised:

  > Let no corrupting talk come out of your mouths, but only such as is good for building up, as fits the occasion, that it may give grace to those who hear (Ephesians 4:29).

  When you discipline your words to do just that, you are helping keep your mind disciplined, which in turn helps your body. Remember, this is all about your success. That's the power behind disciplining your words.

- **Discipline of your emotions:** Emotions have a way of overpowering logic. It's a crazy thing, but it happens all the time. The answer is to discipline your emotions so that you can remain in control, withstand temptation, and stay on course.

Paul knew this, for he challenged us:

> Be angry and do not sin; do not let the sun go down on your anger (Ephesians 4:26 ESV).

> Fathers, do not provoke your children to anger, but bring them up in the discipline and instruction of the Lord (Ephesians 6:4 ESV).

 Now You Know:

Replace "I can't survive this" with "I will grow from this." Resilient words help carry you through daily stresses.

Undisciplined emotions are evident in those who live in the past, refuse to forgive, or are quick to rehash grievances from months, years, even decades ago. This anger keeps tensions high, which is simply extra stress.

Let it go! Concentrate on the demands of the moment and forget about the gripes and grudges of yesterday. Choose to live with kindness, compassion, and forgiveness. Discipline your emotions to be at peace. Flood your heart and mind with positive affirmational and strengthening thoughts and feelings.

HOW TO APPLY SOLITUDE

Just as strength and discipline can increase your resilience, so can solitude. Solitude is all about:

- stepping forward;
- asking questions, finding answers;
- being open, honest, humble;
- communicating with yourself;
- focusing on what is true, not imagined;

- being grateful and;
- accepting people.

Isolation is a bad "attempt" to cope socially and emotionally with the real world. It only prolongs a problem, and usually makes it worse by increasing your sensitivity to a problem.

In fact, isolation and loneliness are as harmful to our health as cigarette smoking (heart disease, stroke, and a weakened immune system).[2,3] All the while, isolation is stealing your opportunities to connect with others at the time when you need them the most.

The expectation, of course, is that isolation will keep the uncomfortable and painful away. But ignoring or avoiding fear, panic, and worry does not make them go away. The only way to really address an issue is to deal with it head on, and that requires the resilience found in practicing solitude.

Solitude is not a lonely place because in true solitude you may be physically alone, but you are totally at ease with the company you keep. It is good for you. It is healthy. And it is purposeful.

 Now You Know:

When you hit a wall, use your resilience tools of strength, humility, and solitude to explore what went awry, make the changes, and try again.

If you grew up using isolation to protect you from dysfunctional, violent, abusive people, it can be easy to slide into old isolating habits. Then when new trauma strikes, bad memories time travel you back to that bad place, and that multiplies the damage of your new injury because you are dealing with the combined pains of your past.

The prophet Elijah repeatedly sought isolation when King Abab's troops were trying to kill him. He hid under a tree, and then twice hid in a cave, convincing himself his troubles were too big to conquer. While in the cave he was visited by the Lord, who asked him, "What are you doing here, Elijah?" to which Elijah responded with a rant of fearful excuses about being alone and powerless. Like a caring friend who shakes us out of our self-pity, the Lord encouraged Elijah to stop isolating and get on with his life's work. It's a powerful story worth reading: 1 Kings 17-19.

Paul spent a lot of time in solitude. After his experience on the road to Damascus, he spent three years in Arabia:

> I did not go up to Jerusalem to see those who were apos-
> tles before I was, but I went into Arabia. Later I returned
> to Damascus (Galatians 1:17).

For Paul, solitude probably included studying scripture, praying, thinking, listening, and writing. That's most likely when much of his writing took place.

In solitude, you are never alone, never isolated, and never lonely. That is because God is always with you. "Do not fear, for I am with you" (Isaiah 41:10 NIV). And He is at work in you, building you up, making you stronger.

If you are unsure about how to start practicing solitude, then try these:

- Schedule time for solitude.
- Take a long walk.
- Sit in a park or in a place of worship.
- Eliminate distractions, especially your phone.
- Seek silence.
- Have a conversation with God where you listen more than talk.

Add solitude to your resilience.

HOW TO APPLY HUMILITY

Humility, in addition to strength, discipline, and solitude, is a powerful part of your resilience. Rest assured, humility is not a sign of weakness. Not in the slightest.

I've heard it said that "the truly great are truly humble," and that is the absolute truth. And I would add that the truly successful, truly free, and truly whole are also truly humble.

That is because humility remains focused on the prize. And if you need to tweak or improve something, you do it. No fighting. No arguing. Just nimble redirection toward the target.

When it comes to trauma and all that goes with it, humility:

- understands that trauma is the exception, not the rule;
- learns from others who have journeyed down similar difficult roads;
- accepts honest criticism;
- celebrates the accomplishments of others;
- respects and values others;
- remains grateful;
- lets go of grudges.

Paul said:

> Do nothing out of selfish ambition or vain conceit. Rather, in humility value others above yourselves (Philippians 2:3 NIV).

 Now You Know:

But humility never accepts injustice or abuse. Respect is always required of self and of others.

The usual sacrifice of humility is that of postponing our personal gratification of the moment. There are times when we fight for a cause that is bigger than ourselves. We may fight for principles of freedom, for the protection of a loved one, or to rescue another in danger, even if we risk our own life.

That is the greatest form of humility.

One of the clearest signs of humility is the trait of gratefulness, and Paul repeatedly preached the importance of gratitude:

- giving joyful thanks (Colossians 1:12)
- overflowing with thankfulness (Colossians 2:7)
- being thankful (Colossians 3:15)

Even in the midst of betrayal and trauma, Paul focused on his gratitude when he wrote from his prison cell:

> I thank my God every time I remember you (Philippians 1:3 NRSV).

If Paul focused only on his traumas, he would have few earthly reasons for gratitude, but he saw gratitude where others could not because he was so incredibly aware of his blessings.

Here is his three-part recipe:

Part #1: Recall your blessings, not your burdens.
Part #2: Keep stress in perspective.
Part #3: Start and end each day with a prayer of gratitude.

Paul understood he was part of something much bigger than his own mortal self. He believed his temporary sufferings meant little in the grander scheme. In his humility, he accepted the mission assigned to him and chose not to complain.

Humility is a vital part of your resilience because it builds your confidence, strengthens you for the inevitable challenges to come, and is essential on the road to recovery.

So embrace it. Make it a part of you, and you will be glad you did.

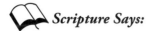
Scripture Says:

Seek these on your own and read them: Job 38:1-41; Proverbs 12:15 and 15:33; Luke14:11; Colossians 3:12; Ephesians 4:2; 1 Peter 5:6-7.

HOW TO APPLY GOALS

Goals—in addition to strength, discipline, solitude, and humility—is the last necessary part of your resilience.

Your first goal then is to define your goals.

T. E. Lawrence (aka Lawrence of Arabia) gave great advice on the value of big dreams:

> All men dream, but not equally. Those who dream by night in the dusty recesses of their minds, wake in the day to find that it was vanity: but the dreamers of the day are dangerous men, for they may act on their dreams with open eyes, to make them possible.[4]

You are free to chart your own course, to set your own goals, but whatever your goals, make sure they are big enough to get you up in the morning. Big goals help you overcome big obstacles.

Regarding goals:

- Goals give you purpose.
- Goals are not based on feelings.
- Goals take you beyond doubt and anxiety.
- Goals give you strength through turmoil.
- Goals make you stronger, able to tolerate pain, ambiguity, disease, disappointment, physical exhaustion, and stress.

Talk over your goals only with those who care and whom you trust. Listen to their feedback and make changes where you need to. When we write down our goals and declare them to others, we are far more likely to achieve them. But above all, make your goal *your* goal. You have to own it and commit to it.

One of Paul's goals was to give "glory and praise to God" (Philippians 1:11). Throughout years of preaching, his goal was to bring others to faith. He would say, "I press on toward the goal to win the prize for which God has called me" (Philippians 3:14 NIV).

Once you know what it is you want, the next step is to make the necessary plans to achieve your goal.

Plans are simply the practical and important steps necessary to achieve your goal. If the plan doesn't take you to your goal, it is an unnecessary distraction. Drop it.

Strategies are the day-to-day building blocks that feed your plans. They must be adaptable to the inevitable hurdles you will face. Adapt where you must, but always with an eye to your plan and goal.

 Now You Know:

Big goals build big resilience by multiplying your courage and your endurance.

Taking these little strategic steps is often the time where people get distracted. Resist that temptation and stay focused. Every strategy, every plan accomplished moves you closer and closer to achieving your big goals.

After nursing school, my mom worked in a hospital while pursuing her goal of getting a college degree. In her plan, she intended to take several courses, but she had to delay her plans while she raised eleven children. The goal and plan remained; the strategies had to adapt. Decades later, after my dad died, she went back and finished her degree.

Pursue your goals, not your anxiety. Daily, step-by-step, you are making progress. Stay on course. Trust your plan. Every day is a battle, and sometimes life is tough, but the goals you are pursuing are yours!

Keep at it.

❋ ❋ ❋

Every day that you can strengthen your resilience means a better tomorrow. You are building strength, adding discipline, using solitude, walking in humility, and working toward your goals.

That is an unstoppable combination!

Chapter 6

Step #2—Arm Yourself with Resistance

One morning back when I was in high school, I was sitting in the dining room eating breakfast when I heard my mom scream. My chair went flying backward as I rushed into the living room.

My dad was standing over my mom. He had shoved her down onto the couch and was taking an aggressive step toward her.

I jumped between them while shouting, "No! You are not going to do this!"

He shoved me aside, gave my mom and me an angry look, and stomped out of the house.

That experience really shook me up. I was a mess of mixed emotions: confused, angry, scared, lost, disappointed.

My mom promptly took my siblings to live at my grandmother's house for a few days, but I stayed at home.

When my dad returned, he asked where everyone was. I told him.

Then he asked me why I was still there, and I said, "In case you wanted to talk."

He never did. In fact, neither that day nor any day since did my dad and I ever speak about that incident.

BUILDING RESISTANCE IS A CHOICE

Resistance is required in the battle. Without resistance, we are overwhelmed, knocked down, defeated, and even destroyed. This is where and when trauma hits: your child was just diagnosed with advanced cancer, your ex-spouse vowed to destroy you financially during a divorce, you were caught with drugs and sentenced to prison. And more. And worse.

You must be well armed, to survive whatever trauma life is going to throw at you.

Did you know that trauma actually hits us more than once? It hits us once when it first happens, and then it hits us again during all the replayed memories and accompanying anxieties.

In both instances, resistance is a choice.

- In the first wave of trauma, fear is very real. You may not be able to prevent the trauma or the fear, but your resistance is needed.
- In the second wave after the trauma, you have to fight against the memories and fear. Resist, no matter how long it takes. Don't let the memories defeat you.

Because resistance is a choice; it is *your* choice. You get to choose. And that means you are building your success, step by step, choice by choice.

Here are the four choices that make up your resistance:
1. Choose courage (over fear);
2. Choose to fight (over quitting);
3. Choose community (over alienation);
4. Choose to be vigilant (over vulnerable).

PAUL HAD NEAR-DEATH EXPERIENCES

When Paul entered a new town, sometimes he was welcomed, sometimes the reaction was mixed, and other times he faced violent hostility. When the people were hostile, he was often brutally attacked before he could escape. He wrote, "But Jews came from Antioch and Iconium, and having won over the crowds, they stoned Paul and dragged him out of the city, supposing him to be dead" (Acts 14:19).

Being beaten and left for dead definitely meets the definition of a major traumatic experience! Vivid details of surviving a near-death experience can lead to PTSD.

But Paul's interpretation of the stoning showed he would not succumb to traumatic stress. He resisted the traumatic stress by courageously embracing suffering as meaningful to his life and mission. Where others might wither, Paul grew stronger.

RESISTANCE THROUGH COURAGE

I don't think all courage comes naturally. We have to learn it, nurture it, and practice it. That's how it's built. Then we are more ready to apply it.

Mark Twain used to say: "Courage is resistance to fear, the mastery of fear—not the absence of fear."

There are many different situations where courage is required, such as:

- when we knowingly and willfully choose to act even when the risk to our own life and limb is great;
- when we fight for a cause, even one that may not come to fruition for generations;

- when we choose a more difficult path for a moral or ethical purpose;
- when we intentionally train for a future moment when courage will be needed.

Usually, courage is summoned in an unplanned crisis, but the more you can be prepared in advance, the better your outcome will be.

Paul's list of traumas, as we've mentioned already, is truly mind boggling. A few that illustrate his courage include:

1. being lowered out a window during the night in a basket to escape being murdered;
2. floating in the open sea for a day and a half;
3. being stoned and left for dead, but returning to the temple to continue preaching;
4. awaiting, in a Roman prison, his death by decapitation.

In the first three situations, Paul courageously chose to live despite the risks so that he could continue his mission. In the Roman prison, however, he could have saved his own life by recanting his beliefs, but that would have undermined everything he taught and believed. Paul chose the certainty of death over the temporary comfort of life.

How did one person have so much courage?

Paul grew up learning about courage. After all, courage is mentioned over 100 times in the Bible and references to "not fear" occur over 300 times. He heard about it, and that helps, but it's not enough.

Paul knew all the Bible stories, especially the one about Joshua being told three times to "be strong and courageous" (Joshua 1:6-9 NIV) as he stepped into leadership after Moses had died. But while knowing real examples is motivating, it is not enough.

PAUL HAD THE COURAGE TO RESIST

Prisoners of war know that their survival depends on their ability to resist. They keep their courage at all costs. Paul faced assaults, imprisonments, arrests, starvations, and more, but he would not allow any force of evil to break him. Paul relied on the same belief he taught Timothy: "For God gave us a spirit not of fear but of power and love and self-control" (2 Timothy 1:7 ESV).

The threats against Paul were very real, but he kept on teaching even when he knew the painful results. His heart, mind, and behavior were all laser-focused on his mission, which fed his courage.

Paul was human. He needed encouragement. One night, while locked in jail, he got it! "The following night the Lord stood near Paul and said, 'Take courage! As you have testified about me in Jerusalem, so you must also testify in Rome'" (Acts 23:11 NIV).

We may not be in jail, but the message to "take courage" applies to all of us.

Take courage!

I think it was his battlefield commission (where a junior officer is instantly elevated in rank when the senior officer is killed) that shook Paul to his core. Everything else was secondary to that.

On the road to Damascus, Jesus told him to stop persecuting Christians, Paul made a choice. From that day forward, he became a leader of the persecuted, and that meant he would be persecuted as well.

Paul knew exactly what he was fighting for, and it was worth everything.

For you and me, we may not have a battlefield commission moment or be faced with life-or-death situations, but we still have plenty to fight for!

We should all ask ourselves:

- What am I fighting for?
- What gives me the courage to resist trauma's control?
- How can I fight my fear with courage?

 Now You Know:

Courage is conquering fear and taking the necessary action despite your fear. Cowardice is giving in to fear and allowing it to rule you, decide for you, and control you.

Maybe you are fighting back against your abusers because you want a new life. Maybe you are fighting addictions, so you can save your family. Maybe you are fighting inner battles, so you can be free and whole.

Whatever the case may be, keep your courage. Resist defeat. You are worth fighting for!

It's difficult to maintain continuous courage. We all have a breaking point. I have had my share and have fallen many times, sometimes because of others and sometimes because of my own self. But as they say:

> "It's not getting knocked down that determines our future, it's getting back up that matters."

South African leader Nelson Mandela spent 27 years in prison. He later said, "I learned that courage is not the absence of fear, but the triumph over it. The brave man is not he who does not feel afraid, but he who conquers it."

Choose resistance through courage.

RESISTANCE THROUGH FIGHTING

We all face battles, whether they are current threats or past ones that affect the present. Whatever the threat, fighting to win is the only option.

Clearly, there are things worth fighting for, and *you* are highest on that list. No matter how you feel, no matter how great your stress, no matter your ability, you are worth it.

Maybe it's a fight:

- to overcome the desire to stay in bed all day;
- to save a struggling marriage;
- to engage with your children;
- to deal with private emotional struggles;
- to control your trauma triggers;
- to remain patient;
- to forgive your ex.

Whatever the fight, you know that quitting is not an option. Yes, it might be difficult, but difficult is not impossible!

Say "no" to anxiety and worry.
They only slow you down.
Say "no" to depression.
That is a slippery slope.
Say "no" to suicide.
That is never, ever, the answer.
Say "no" to pride and arrogance.
They get you off track.
Say "no" to escape through addictions.
Those just delay your healing.

Why are you fighting anyway? Because you want victory! You want to be whole again. You want to be fully alive. You want to be connected and present in the moment. You want to be free of everything that holds you back.

While you are building up your resistance through fighting, be careful that you don't fall into the trap of anger. Paul was very aware, for he used to teach:

 Now You Know:

Lose your temper and you lose control. As Eleanor Roosevelt has been quoted saying, "anger" is one letter short of "danger."

> Be angry and do not sin; do not let the sun go down on your anger, and give no opportunity to the devil (Ephesians 4:26–27 ESV).

Being angry is one thing, but letting that anger have its way is another issue entirely. Here are three dangers to consider and avoid:

1. Being angry does not make you right.
2. Feeling anger is not a sufficient reason to fight.
3. Venting anger does not make it good.

Anger has a way of blinding your ability to see reason, turning off your compassion, sidetracking you back to old symptoms, and making you lose sight of your positive purpose. That is not good for you at all!

The bottom line with anger is that anger will not help you in your fight against trauma.

Choose to fight, but leave anger out of it.

RESISTANCE THROUGH COMMUNITY

If you have felt the sting of abandonment or abuse, you know how bad it can hurt. And being alone in the middle of a fight makes it all that much harder. You need a team on your side.

We are social beings at heart and need the companionship of others. That is where community comes in, whether it's family, friends, coworkers, classmates, teams, or a congregation.

For those who experience trauma early in life, attachment to others and a community is particularly difficult. Relationships may trigger fears of abandonment, feelings of unworthiness, an insatiable drive to prove your worthiness, and intense self-blame.

Community is the place where we develop safe and sustained relationships to overcome the fears from trauma. The benefits of being part of a community include:

- being healthier, happier, and more stress resilient;
- believing our actions matter to someone;
- greater self-esteem;
- less doubt;
- greater courage;
- better health (living longer, lower blood pressure, and lower risk for dementia).

Fighting through trauma is easier when you are in good company. Without those valued relationships, loneliness is not far behind. Interestingly, people hospitalized for heart disease are three times more likely to die within one year of leaving the hospital if they live alone, and those who describe themselves as lonely are three times more likely to report feeling anxious and depressed.[1] What's more, impaired social relationships are associated with both a higher risk for and impaired recovery from PTSD.[2]

Community is good for you!

The most common causes of "not enough" community include:

Feeling forgotten: Moving, taking a new job, changing careers, retiring, and getting divorced. The change may be good, but the change also disrupts the normal patterns within a community, and the tendency is to feel forgotten.

Feeling neglected: A new student on campus, empty-nester parents with no kids at home, grandparents with few visitors, and those in prison can feel neglected.

Feeling lost: Those who have lost a spouse or parent through death or divorce can feel lost.

Feeling lonely: Homeless people, the spouse of a military service member waiting out the deployment, the grieving widow, and the worker who must be away from home for months on end can be lonely.

Feeling forsaken: This happens when others deliberately reject us and stay away, for whatever reason. This also includes public shunning on social media.

Feeling bullied: The bullied are actively attacked. Be it prejudice, bigotry, grudges, or anger, the goal is to destroy the other person.

In the wake of trauma, we often feel alienated, betrayed, and abandoned. We can slip into convincing ourselves we are the least, lost, and lonely. But that is not the case at all!

Paul was forgotten, forsaken, and bullied for many years, but his endurance was strengthened by the core belief that he was never alone. He knew by heart:

> Have I not commanded you? Be strong and courageous!
> Do not tremble or be dismayed, for the Lord your God is
> with you wherever you go (Joshua 1:9 NASB).

PAUL WAS SHIPWRECKED (PART 1)

Paul had appealed to Caesar, so he was sent to Rome on a ship with other prisoners, crew, soldiers, and his friend, Luke. They battled dangerous winds and strong currents for several days with little progress. Paul warned that disaster awaited them at sea and pleaded with the centurion guard to wait out the winter season in the safety of harbor, but the centurion and ship owner chose not to. On a day when the winds appeared to calm, they set sail from a harbor in Crete. Trouble quickly followed.

Before very long, a wind of hurricane force, called the Northeaster, swept down from the island. The ship was caught by the storm and could not head into the wind; so we gave way to it and were driven along. As we passed to the lee of a small island called Cauda, we were hardly able to make the lifeboat secure, so the men hoisted it aboard. Then they passed ropes under the ship itself to hold it together. Because they were afraid they would run aground on the sandbars of Syrtis, they lowered the sea anchor and let the ship be driven along. We took such a violent battering from the storm that the next day they began to throw the cargo overboard. On the third day, they threw the ship's tackle overboard with their own hands. When neither sun nor stars appeared for many days and the storm continued raging, we finally gave up all hope of being saved (Acts 27:14-20 NIV).

Yes, sometimes people will abandon you. It happens. But you are never alone and that is never the end. Paul proclaimed his own source of strength to resist feelings of abandonment when he wrote:

We are afflicted in every way, but not constrained; perplexed, but not driven to despair; persecuted; but not abandoned; struck down, but not destroyed (2 Corinthians 4:8-9 NAB).

The right attitude or mindset is that of being an overcomer, no matter what situation you are in. Remember, symptoms do not prove anything. You may have been abandoned, but that never means you deserved it.

Choose resistance by being part of a community.

RESISTANCE THROUGH VIGILANCE

The Buffalo Creek flood in Logan County, West Virginia, ranks as one of the worst dam collapse disasters in US history. Three days of heavy rain caused a series of dams made of coal mine waste to fail. Tens of millions of cubic yards of coal slurry and water, as high as 30 feet, rushed down the narrow valley for three hours, devastating 17 towns and demolishing 500 homes. The destruction left 4,000 people homeless, 1,000 injured and 125 dead.

As a young college kid, I volunteered to help victims. The local high school was set up as a temporary shelter. There I asked one of the survivors if his family was safe.

With a raspy, tired voice barely above a whisper he said, "Yes." Then he added, "They're safe. Others gone."

He spoke slowly, deliberately, emotionless, in his West Virginia mountain accent, pausing between each sentence: "I was on my porch when I heard the police car siren. The policeman shouted, 'The dam broke. Run.' I grabbed my wife and kids and told them to run up the hill. The water came real loud down the holler. As fast as I ran, the water was right behind my feet. When I got up high, I turned around. My house and all our neighbors' houses were floating down the creek, falling apart in slow motion like they was made of sticks or sumpthin."

He added, "One of my neighbors was up at the store when it hit. His whole family was in their house. They all died. He lived."

After several moments, I broke the silence: "Your family is lucky."

"Luck ain't got nothin' to do with it, son," he corrected me as he leaned forward. "We both knew it was gonna happen. We both got the same warning." Then he sat back again and stared out as if talking to himself. "I listened. He didn't. That's the difference. His family is gone. Mine is alive." He softly repeated, "I listened," then turned away and lay down to sleep.

I maintain vivid memories of that conversation. There are signs out there of our own vulnerabilities surrounding us, and within us. We better be vigilant, we better listen, or else "vulnerable" can quickly turn to "victim."

To be vigilant is to be honestly aware of where you are vulnerable (inside or outside) that might hurt you in any way.

For example, knowing what may trigger you, cause anxiety, ruin your sleep, or mess with your stomach is very important. Then you deal with each situation with honesty, which directly increases your chances of winning.

This is a battle, for where our minds go, our hearts will follow. It's always that way. Without vigilance, we will keep falling back into the traps of misery, self-pity, and depression.

Sun Tzu, in *The Art of War*, insightfully noted:

> That general is skillful in attack whose opponent does not know what to defend.[3]

How true! If we are ignorant of our own vulnerabilities, then it's virtually impossible to be vigilant, on guard, and able to defend ourselves.

But you are aware. You know. That's why we are here. You are getting more and more equipped to resist!

PAUL WAS SHIPWRECKED (PART 2)

Paul tried to assure the crew and prisoners they would be safe. But as the storms raged, this little ship barely held together, and they had long ago lost the means to steer it.

After two weeks in the storm, the soldiers aboard the ship tried to escape in a lifeboat and abandon the passengers on board, but Paul convinced the centurion to make the soldiers stay.

On the fourteenth night we were still being driven across the Adriatic Sea, when about midnight the sailors sensed they were approaching land. They took soundings and found that the water was a hundred and twenty feet deep. A short time later they took soundings again and found it was ninety feet deep. Fearing that we would be dashed against the rocks, they dropped four anchors from the stern and prayed for daylight. In an attempt to escape from the ship, the sailors let the lifeboat down into the sea, pretending they were going to lower some anchors from the bow. Then Paul said to the centurion and the soldiers, "Unless these men stay with the ship, you cannot be saved." So the soldiers cut the ropes that held the lifeboat and let it drift away (Acts 27: 27-32 NIV).

When they finally spotted land, they sailed for the beach. While still a good distance from shore, however, their ship ran aground and broke apart in the waves. They had no choice but to jump overboard and swim to shore.

Here is a checklist of twelve common obstacles on the way toward the mental, emotional, and spiritual freedom that you want:

The Killer Ds: How we try to fool ourselves that we have cured our vulnerability

1. **Deny the problem exists:** This is thinking, "If I do not even speak the name of my problem, I don't have to deal with it. It never happened."

2. **Dismiss the need for help:** This is saying, "It's not that big of a deal. Talking about this with someone won't make a difference. They don't know what they are talking about anyway."

3. **Distort:** This is like saying, "I don't have PTSD, I'm just tired." Or "I don't need to see a doctor to tell this is skin cancer, it's just a mole." Or "I'm not alcoholic, I just like to drink."

4. **Deceive:** This is like saying, "I'm this way because God's punishing me." Or "I can still eat these snacks today and go on my diet tomorrow." Or "I think the 'check engine' light that came on is actually broken, not the car." "Others are to blame not me."

5. **Despair:** This is thinking, "I just can't shake this. I'm stuck. My life is pointless. I always fail, so why try? I've been at this so long, I can't stop. I am too hurt to heal."

6. **Distract:** This is staying too busy to do what is needed. Overwhelm yourself with work.

7. **Drugs:** This includes alcohol, drugs, binge eating, candy, and even the adrenalin rush of risky activities.

8. **Deflect:** This is saying, "It's not my problem, it's everyone else. When they change, I'll be happy."

9. **Discontent:** This is turning anxiety and depression into anger and agitation, sad into mad, and anger into violence.

10. **Detach:** This is thinking, "I'm not really here. I'm watching all of this like I'm in a movie. I have no feelings."

11. **Done:** This is prematurely saying, "It will never happen again. This is fixed."

12. **Death:** This is thinking, "This pain will never stop. I'm better off dead"

PAUL WAS SHIPWRECKED (PART 3)

Act continues:

When daylight came, they did not recognize the land, but they saw a bay with a sandy beach, where they decided to run the ship aground if they could. Cutting loose the anchors, they left them in the sea and at the same time untied the ropes that held the rudders. Then they hoisted the foresail to the wind and made for the beach. But the ship struck a sandbar and ran aground. The bow stuck fast and would not move, and the stern was broken to pieces by the pounding of the surf. The soldiers planned to kill the prisoners to prevent any of them from swimming away and escaping. But the centurion wanted to spare Paul's life and kept them from carrying out their plan. He ordered those who could swim to jump overboard first and get to land. The rest were to get there on planks or on other pieces of the ship. In this way everyone reached land safely (Acts 27:39-44 NIV).

Although no one perished on Paul's boat, modern research would predict that the fight for survival over two stormy weeks adrift at sea, hungry, with threats of being murdered by the soldiers, and many sleepless nights must have had a traumatic impact on many of those onboard.

But there were no indications of such a reaction from Paul. He kept right on going. And right in the middle of it, he stayed true to his beliefs.

Being aware is the first step toward change. With vigilance, you render these twelve "Killer Ds" null and void in your life.

Paul knew this to be the case as well. One often-memorized scripture states:

> Keep your heart with all vigilance, for from it flow the springs of life (Proverbs 4:23 ESV).

Fighting back requires constant vigilance. The more you know, the more you are aware; and the more you address each situation honestly, the greater your success will be.

That is inevitable.

For Paul, his vigilance was crucial to keeping his own reactions to trauma under control. He was aware of robbers and thieves on the roads he traveled and of the continual risks of being stoned, whipped, jailed, and executed. He also knew his own weaknesses, one of which he metaphorically referred to as the "thorn" in his flesh (2 Corinthians 12:6).

Paul took his vigilance a few steps further. When he was in pain, he did not dwell on the suffering. Instead, he transformed his weakness into strength, declaring:

> That is why, for the sake of Christ, I delight in weaknesses, in insults, in hardships, in persecutions, in difficulties. For when I am weak, then I am strong (2 Corinthians 12:10 BSB).

Choose to remain vigilant.

❋ ❋ ❋

Resistance is always a choice, so keep fighting forward, armed with:

1. Your courage, not fear;
2. Your fighting, not quitting;
3. Your community, not alienation;
4. Your vigilance; not vulnerablity.

Chapter 7

How to Apply Your Resistance

Katryn remembers only fragments from the incident when she was twelve years old, because she was unconscious much of the time. In her own words she was "assaulted in multiple, unspeakable ways" by a stranger.

Being unconscious may have saved her life as the perpetrator left her for dead. When she awoke, she managed to make it home in the cold November afternoon and tell her mother what had happened.

Incredibly, her unsympathetic mother called her a "liar" and a "family embarrassment" and commanded her to never speak about it again.

What rescued her from her nightmares was her loving dad, who would hold her in the evenings until she cried herself to sleep. He whispered in her ear, "I'm so sorry. I wish I could have prevented this. You are good. Don't ever feel ashamed. I love you."

He also explained that her mother was sick (suffering from what they called "manic depression" back in those days) and often did not know what she was doing or saying.

Katryn did not tell him that her mother also locked her in the dark garage for hours at a time, telling her, "You belong with the garbage." Out of fear of even worse punishment, Katryn said nothing.

To fight back against the trauma, whether alone in the garage or while battling her nightmares, Katryn comforted herself by remembering her father's words: that she was good, she was not to blame, and she was loved.

Katryn could not erase the trauma of the past, but she fought back by refusing to let the "garbage" label stick. She refused to let her memories of yesterday morph into tormenting demons of tomorrow.

Today, she keeps on winning because she keeps on fighting. That is courage in action, and that is how she applies her resistance.

YOU GET TO CHOOSE

Whether your trauma is a current reality or a painful past, you must continue to fight back. Quitting is never an option. Rest assured that you can and will overcome the pain.

Do you have your own mental demons of grieving, loneliness, depression, feelings of worthlessness, or wishing to die? Or maybe it's a battle against addiction, disease, chronic pain, a broken heart, abuse, lack of finances, or another item on the limitless list of possibilities.

We all have trauma in one form or another. Whatever your situation might be, you always get to choose how you will respond. Will it be to fight or to quit? Will it be courage or fear?

Courageously fight back. That is to resist.

And that is the path to freedom.

HOW TO APPLY COURAGE

Resistance offers you many different ways to achieve the freedom and peace that you seek. It begins with the foundational choice to have courage.

Several years ago, I had the honor of meeting Aung San Suu Kyi, the prime minister of Myanmar, while visiting her country. Her courageous stance on behalf of human rights is legendary. For her acts of defiance against massive repression in her country, the controlling military regime kept her under house arrest for the majority of 20 years, or she was imprisoned with hard labor.

She never wavered. She always spoke up on behalf of the people of Myanmar and the hardships they have endured. She has written and said a great deal about fear, but this one has always stood out to me:

"The only real prison is fear, and the only freedom is freedom from fear."[1]

 Now You Know:

Courage is built wherever and whenever it is tested and fear is conquered.

Clearly, we must all choose courage over fear. Regardless of what we may face, courage is the answer. Fear is never a good option.

Of course, it's easier said than done. That's why it's such an important choice to make. Courage is the right option, but you must first choose it.

Courage is undeniably necessary in times of war, but it's far more commonly needed in the little day-to-day decisions that you need to make. That includes relationships, talking, working through differences, raising children, growing in your profession, and so much more.

Every part of life requires courage. I've seen incredibly skilled soldiers buckle under the demands of a relationship or a home.

It's not about the specific thing that someone faces, it's about choosing to face whatever it is courageously. Big or little, courage is needed.

And big or little, if you happen to fail to have courage in an area, rest assured that failure is not permanent. Courage takes practice. So don't worry about it. Just keep moving forward.

Now, I have found that practicing courage means I can't live the life of a recluse. I have to get up and face the world. And life will give me plenty of opportunities each and every day to choose courage.

The same is true for you.

Every challenge you face is an opportunity to reinforce courage or fear. Practice it by your actions and in your mind, especially in your mind. You can mentally rehearse many more challenges and courageous victories than you could ever experience, and that is good practice.

When facing challenges, I like to meditate on Bible truths, such as:

> Though an army besiege me, my heart will not fear; though war break out against me, even then I will be confident (Psalm 27:3).

Courage builds confidence, and confidence has a way of building more courage. It does not have to be tested in warfare. Even little steps in the right direction are powerful.

I often challenge people who are focusing on building their courage to do one hundred small selfless acts over as many days at it takes to do them. Then count them as they go: opening the door for someone, paying for the person behind you at the coffee shop, donating old clothes to a charity, volunteering, encouraging someone, and so on.

The point is, every single selfless act is an act of courage, and all combined, that's one hundred small steps in the right direction!

That's a lot. And once you start looking, you will find countless other little ways to practice courage.

Here is a courage checklist we can all keep handy:

✓ **The biggest fight is usually internal:** Am I speaking the truth about myself? Do I really care what others say about me? Am I accepting responsibility? Do I give and accept forgiveness?

✓ **Children need a leader:** Am I the person I want my kids to be? Do I model the courage to ask for help? Am I mentoring them to make the right choices?

✓ **Catch others doing good:** Do I support those who are doing what is right? Do I notice? Do I compliment them? Do I foster an environment around me of doing good?

✓ **Start the day out right:** Do I remind myself every morning that I can face the difficulties of the day? Do I focus on what is worthy and honorable, pray for courage, not run from what is difficult, and head into each day with courageous confidence?

✓ **Improvement is constant:** Do I push myself in my fitness, diet, and mental health to be stronger? Am I looking for ways to get better in every area of life?

✓ **Stand up for what is right:** Do I know when to walk away and when to stand up for what is right? Am I willing to do what it takes? Do I watch out for others as well as myself?

✓ **Say "no thank you" to temptation:** Do I avoid situations that tempt me (like drinking after work, getting into needless debt, spending time with the wrong people, listening to negative voices)? Do I look for ways to lock the door before it even cracks open?

✓ **Ask others for help:** Am I willing, without getting mad or depressed, to ask for help? Do I look for ways to use courage to fight against nightmares, broken relationships, and anxiety?

✓ **Resilience is needed:** Do I courageously stand up to my fears? Am I willing to let go of victimhood? Do I use my stress and trauma as stepping stones to my recovery?

When it comes to checklists, I have found the best advice is less talking and more doing. We are all very talented at talking ourselves out of our own courage. The remedy is to simply get up and do it.

Doing good constantly is in itself an act of courage. Paul knew that when he wrote, "And let us not grow weary of doing good, for in due season we will reap, if we do not give up" (Galatians 6:9 ESV). He knew that if you hang in there and keep at it, you will eventually win!

"Courage is contagious," Rev. Billy Graham used to say. "When a brave man takes a stand, the spines of others are stiffened." It's true, no matter where your realm of influence might be."[2]

Life is a battle. And your courage is absolutely necessary and absolutely possible.

Theodore Roosevelt noted, "Nothing in life is worth having or worth doing unless it means effort, pain, difficulty . . . I have never in my life envied a human being who led an easy life; I have envied a great many people who led difficult lives and led them well."

Isn't that the truth?

So let's be those who lead lives well.

 Scripture Says:

Read these: Gideon's choice of courage over fear: Judges Chapter 6; and David's courage in 1 Samuel 17:32–37.

HOW TO APPLY FIGHTING

In addition to courage, resistance through fighting is how you get the freedom you want. Fighting back, like courage, is a choice. It's certainly a given: you must fight to get what you want! Do not be passive against temptations and torment. Don't let them defeat you.

The need to fight, to fight forward inch by inch for the life you want, is a necessity. But the more specific your reason for fighting, the better. You see, when trauma hits, or in the aftershock of post-traumatic stress, knowing why you are fighting back gives you incredible resolve and unflinching determination.

Fueled by a strong reason to fight, you will press forward. You will not be denied!

As you fight forward, apply these fighting principles:

#1—Fight by enduring. Fighting takes time and demands effort, and that is why it requires endurance. Weariness will come. I know what it feels like to think, "How much longer? This pain has gone on too long. There is no end in sight."

That's an awful feeling, but it's normal. It's part of the process. Endurance is your defense in the battle. During those times when your mind is screaming at you and your body is tired, hang in there. You can endure a little longer.

Paul knew what endurance felt like, and he knew it was part of life. That's why he taught, "No temptation has overtaken you that is not common to man. God is faithful, and he will not let you be tempted beyond your ability, but with the temptation he will also provide the way of escape, that you may be able to endure it" (1 Corinthians 10:13 ESV).

Your driving purpose increases your ability to endure. That's why meaningless suffering is hard to tolerate, while the same pain as the price for victory is much easier to endure.

For example, Marine recruits (after a four-month boot camp) endure the Crucible, which is a 54-hour intensive test of mind, body, spirit, and emotion that includes 48 miles of marching, 36 stations-testing skills learned in boot camp, 29 team-building exercises, and all this with only six hours of sleep and two meals. Why? It's the willingly accepted price of becoming a Marine!

PAUL PRACTICED ENDURANCE

Paul did not identify suffering as surprising, strange, or overwhelming. No matter how much was thrown at him, he used his painful experiences to inspire endurance, not to complain.

In this way, Paul's suffering created compassion, bringing his followers a little closer to understanding what kind of love Jesus must have felt in order to endure agony many times greater than anything we would face. When someone lays down their life for us, we know their love is genuine and total. In a similar way, we can reinterpret our own endurance in the healing process as evidence of a commitment to our love for others and ourselves.

Paul wrote, "I pray that out of His glorious riches He may strengthen you with power through His Spirit in your inner being, so that Christ may dwell in your hearts through faith. And I pray that you, being rooted and established in love, may have power, together with all the Lord's holy people, to grasp how wide and long and high and deep is the love of Christ, and to know this love that surpasses knowledge—that you may be filled to the measure of all the fullness of God" (Ephesians 3:16-19 NIV).

#2—**Fight by reframing the pain.** When you reframe the pain, it makes you stronger. To "reframe" something does not make it go away, nor does it mean you pretend it doesn't exist. Not at all. Instead, to reframe something gives it a greater purpose in your life, and as such, you willingly accept it. And you grow, overcome, and surpass it.

Paul certainly understood that one! He is the one who penned these famous words, "We rejoice in our sufferings, knowing that suffering produces endurance, and endurance produces character, and character produces hope, and hope does not put us to shame, because God's love has been poured into our hearts through the Holy Spirit who has been given to us" (Romans 5:2–5 ESV).

He actually said to "rejoice" in suffering! When you reframe the pain, you can see suffering as a means to a positive end. Whatever the pain, be it physical, spiritual, mental or emotional, if you can see the benefit of dealing with it, then the battle is almost over.

Reframing stops procrastination, gives you strength, and helps you see clearly into the future.

Now You Know:

Be careful of the lie that failure is inevitable. The truth is far better— success is a choice!

#3—Fight by persisting. I was sitting in a hospital waiting room once, and across from me sat a mom and her child in his motorized wheelchair. He was severely disabled, unable to talk or care for himself. She told me he was just seven years old, but was here for his 33rd surgery! I asked if she needed anything. "Prayers," she replied. "We can always use more prayers." She understood they both needed help to persist.

To beat back internal and external demons, persistence is required. Paul understood that: "Not that I have already obtained all of this, or have already arrived at my goal, but I press on to take hold of that for which Christ Jesus took hold of me" (Philippians 3:12 NIV). To press on is to persist. That is how Paul pushed himself, always focused, always persevering towards the long-term goal, while avoiding distractions of his past.

Persistence is your offensive. Triumph goes to the one who persists. That is always the case. Failing and falling are part of life, but staying down is a choice. I like how the well-known Proverb states it: "For though the righteous fall seven times, they rise again, but the wicked stumble when calamity strikes" (Proverbs 26:16 NIV).

It doesn't really matter if you fail. Just get back up one more time. That's the secret to persisting, and that will take you across the finish line.

#4—Fight by throwing off self-pity. Feeling sorry for ourselves distracts us into asking the wrong questions, such as: "Why me? Why do I have to go through this? What if I can't handle this? What did I do to deserve this?" This leads to the arrogance of self-pity, and self-pity is the enemy of persistence.

I knew a mother fighting a chronic disease who took medication to control symptoms and manage pain, but the side effects included a rash, hair falling out in clumps, and intense gut pain. Her finances were strained, she had used up all her sick days at work, and she lived on a special diet. When she would attend her kids' sporting events, other parents avoided her as if she were contagious. With all that against her she chose to use the stares and rejection as fuel to overcome with humility, not allowing their judgmental eyes to make her wallow in self-pity or bitterness.

Your battle may be more internal than external, but it doesn't really matter. You must not let self-pity get a foothold in your life.

#5—Fight by waking up. Make no mistake: it is a fight and it is not easy, but you can do it. You have strength within you to face any battle. Fighting makes you strong!

When you see this, it is as if your eyes are opened and you "wake up" to your reality. Phillips Brooks of Boston, an American Episcopal clergyman and author (and lyricist for the Christmas song "Oh Little Town of Bethlehem), understood this when he said, "Do not pray for easy lives. Pray to be stronger men. Do not pray for tasks equal to your powers. Pray for powers equal to your tasks. Then the doing of your work shall be no miracle, but you shall be the miracle."[3]

You are the miracle! You are far from a helpless victim! When you wake up to this reality, your thinking changes, fears melt into courage, and you see tomorrow in a new light. Press on!

HOW TO APPLY COMMUNITY

The power of community is another tool, besides courage and fighting, that you can use to get the life of freedom you want. It begins by choosing to be part of a community rather than choosing to be alone.

Within a community is the basic understanding that everyone operates by the Golden Rule. It is "love your neighbor as yourself" (Leviticus 19:18) in action.

It is also the place where we push each other, grow together, support each other through our good times and bad.

For Paul, this was indispensable for spiritual growth despite his mistakes and doubts. He wrote, "Brothers and sisters, if someone is caught in a sin, you who live by the Spirit should restore that person gently. But watch yourselves, or you also may be tempted. Carry each other's burdens" (Galatians 6:1–2 NIV).

 Now You Know:

Being part of a community boosts confidence and courage.

Community breeds healthy people, which alone is a good enough reason to be part of a community. Finding others who are committed to your growth, and vice versa, is an incredible thing.

Paul understood well the benefits of a community. His teachings were sprinkled with that reality:

- "Do nothing from rivalry or conceit, but in humility count others more significant than yourselves. Let each of you look not only to his own interests, but also to the interests of others" (Philippians 2:3–4 ESV).
- "We who are strong in faith should help the weak with their weaknesses, and not please only ourselves" (Romans 15:1 NCV).
- "From whom the whole body, joined and held together by every joint with which it is equipped, when each part is working properly, makes the body grow so that it builds itself up in love" (Ephesians 4:16 ESV).
- "As it is, there are many parts, yet one body. The eye cannot say to the hand, 'I do not need you,' nor again the head to the feet, 'I do not need you.' Indeed, the parts of the body that seem to be weaker are all the more necessary, and those parts of the body that we consider less honorable we surround with greater honor, and our less presentable parts are treated with greater propriety, whereas our more presentable parts do not need this. But God has so constructed the body as to give greater honor to a part that is without" (1 Corinthians 12:20–25 NABRE).

We simply need each other! To assume we can do life alone is not smart, efficient, safe, helpful, or loving.

Here is a quick checklist of what to look for in your community:

- ✓ **Look for true friends:** These are more than party friends. True friends will guide you, not let you repeat your crimes, nor tolerate your abuse toward others or yourself. Your healthy community is there to stop you from making mistakes, and rescue you when you do. "A friend loves at all times, and a brother is born for adversity" (Proverbs 17:17 NASB).

✓ **Names don't matter:** Your community could be a group that helps you recover from an addiction. It could be a Bible study group. It could be a veterans' organization. It could be a friend or several friends with whom you can be honest and who can be honest with you.

✓ **Be open to advice and counsel:** Pride and stubbornness will not nurture growth at all, for anyone in the community. Paul was very wise, but he received counsel from many. Humility speeds healing and opens many doors.

✓ **Meet regularly:** Getting together on a regular basis is necessary for connecting and accountability. It also breeds trust and respect. "And let us consider how to stir up one another to love and good works, not neglecting to meet together, as is the habit of some, but encouraging one another, and all the more as you see the day drawing near" (Hebrews 10:24–25 ESV).

✓ **Aim high:** The goal is growth. Seek those you can look up to, not those who will bring you back down. Keep an eye out for mentors who have been victors against their own demons, for their comfort and sound advice is priceless.

If you do not have your community yet, find one. There is always one out there for you.

Sadly, there are times when people will not be there when we need them. During my lowest points, I hesitantly called a few people. Some listened and gave me counsel, but a few rebuffed or ignored me. That hurt! I felt bitter, angry, and even more overwhelmed with shame and self-condemnation than before.

Does that mean we avoid community to protect ourselves from those who might hurt us? That in itself is a lie, but it's also illogical. We would never learn to walk, talk, swim, or ride a bike if we listened to that lie.

Then, to my surprise, a new community seemed to spring up around me. People I knew only a little, some complete strangers, rallied around me. They persisted as true friends do. Together, they offered comfort in affliction, discussed forgiveness, hope, humility, sacrifice and prayer, shared their own struggles, and helped hold up my arms. I even received letters in the mail from people offering encouragement and prayers.

All of these people became my new community. At first I thought I was alone, but that was not the case at all. There were people all around me who were willing to step up and help.

That is community, and they are there for you as well.

HOW TO APPLY VIGILANCE

In addition to courage, fighting, and community, vigilance is another powerful step toward freedom. Vigilance is a choice that requires a combination of awareness and action.

Years ago, I was with the Navy medical crew aboard the *USS George Washington*. One day, I was set to return to San Diego on a C-2 COD (Carrier Onboard Delivery), a small cargo plane that carries a few passengers, mail, and supplies. When it was time to depart, a member of the aircrew gave us our instructions before he guided us to the plane. What he said was the best definition of vigilance I have ever heard.

"Listen up!" he yelled, above the roar of noises around us. "This is for your safety! This is an active flight deck with aircraft landing, taking off, being towed, red hot jet engines, and spinning propellers. I'm going to walk you around these aircraft to your plane, and you will follow me. The man behind me, watch where I walk, the man behind him, watch where he walks. All the way down the line you do exactly what I do. At all times be aware of any danger around you, but follow the steps of person in front of you. Do not get distracted and start looking to the left or right at all the pretty airplanes, because *where your eyes go, your feet follow.* You'll start drifting toward where you are looking, and that's when someone gets hurt. If you step out of line everyone behind you follows you, and they get hurt. You will get sucked into an engine or chopped up by a propeller. I don't want to put you in a bag and write letters home for you. So pay attention! Be vigilant! Clear?"

It could not have been more clear! We obeyed and vigilantly walked that windy deck, alert to the heat of jet blasts, the deafening engine roar, and high-tempo activity around us. Our lives depended on it.

The same principle applies to trauma. Your vigilance is always required. (See Proverbs 4:25-27)

Since Paul and Luke spent so much time together, I suspect Luke shared Jesus's words:

> "Be dressed for action and have your lamps lit; be like those who are waiting for their master to return from the wedding banquet, so that they may open the door for him as soon as he comes and knocks." (Luke 12:35 NRSV)

> "Be on guard so that your hearts are not weighed down . . . Be alert at all times" (Luke 21:34–36 NRSV).

PAUL KNEW THE COST

"If it is serving, then serve; if it is teaching, then teach" (Romans 12:7 NIV). Paul was there to teach. But teaching came at a cost. Each time he taught, he spoke the truth in love, even when he was beaten and left for dead. He would get back up and continue preaching.

Each lesson meant to inspire followers aroused his enemies anew. Each debate brought him closer to arrest and death. Each proclamation strengthened his personal commitment to overcome any flaws, forgive any failures, endure any pain, and dispel any doubt, all with no hesitation.

Teaching recommitted him every day to not succumb to trauma.

Paul understood that, especially with regards to fighting internal battles. These internal battles, between doing what is right and succumbing to sin, are something we can all identify with. He understood he was vulnerable to weakness, temptation, and sin:

> "I do not understand my own actions. For I do not do what I want, but I do the very thing I hate . . . For I know that nothing good dwells within me, that is, in my flesh. I can will what is right, but I cannot do it. For I do not do the good I want, but the evil I do not want is what I do. Now if I do what I do not want, it is no longer I that do it, but sin that dwells within me" (Romans 7:15–20 NRSB).

While constant struggles weaken our will, the stress sets the stage for a desire to escape the pain. Where our heart goes, temptation follows. Where temptation goes, behavior follows. Paul warned us where we need to be on the alert:

> "Now the works of the flesh are obvious: immorality, impurity, licentiousness, idolatry, sorcery, hatreds, rivalry, jealousy, outbursts of fury, acts of selfishness, dissensions, factions, occasions of envy, drinking bouts, orgies, and the like. I warn you, as I warned you before, that those who do such things will not inherit the kingdom of God" (Galatians 5:19–21 NABRE).

And Paul also warned of the consequences if we failed to be vigilant:

> "Nor thieves, nor the greedy, nor drunkards, nor revilers, nor swindlers will inherit the kingdom of God" (1 Corinthians 6:10 ESV).

Paul knew what it meant to be vigilant. His warnings are indeed helpful, but as you know, warnings alone are not enough to keep anyone out of trouble. What is needed is enough personal discipline to set specific goals. Consider these:

- "Set your minds on things that are above, not on things that are on earth" (Colossians 3:2 NRSV).
- "Be on your guard; stand firm in the faith; be courageous; be strong" (1 Corinthians 16:13 NIV).
- "So then let us not sleep, as others do, but let us keep awake and be sober" (1 Thessalonians 5:6 ESV).
- "Examine yourselves, to see whether you are in the faith. Test yourselves" (2 Corinthians 13:5 ESV).

I believe Paul's resistance was a result of his:

1. Mental, physical, emotional, and spiritual strength;
2. Humility to admit his own vulnerabilities;
3. Self-discipline to resist temptations;
4. Remaining focused on clearly defined goals/plans;
5. Remaining on the alert to any vulnerabilities;
6. commitment to courageously press on in the fight.

That's how he fought back against trauma. And that is our example for how we can do the same.

Chapter 8

Step #3—Embrace Your Recovery

I was once helping raise funds for Habitat for Humanity, and we were holding a triathlon for kids. The event involved swimming a few laps, biking one mile, and then running half a mile. No matter where you placed, as long as you finished, you received a medal.

During the race, a dad came up to me with his 10-year-old daughter and pointed at her skinned knee. He explained how she had completed the swim, the bike ride, and half the run, but had hurt her knee and could not continue.

He then asked if his daughter could still get the "finisher's medal."

I could see her knee was scraped, but the way she put weight on her leg and still walked showed me that it was not a serious injury.

"The rules are that only those who finish get a medal," I explained. "I'm sorry, but she has to finish to get the medal."

The dad was mad, and she was embarrassed.

"But she trained so hard," he complained.

I pointed out, "She obviously has a determined spirit, but training isn't finishing. Quitting isn't finishing. Finishing is what counts."

While he continued to argue, I turned to the girl and asked, "Can you walk?"

"Yes," she replied.

"Can you walk the last lap?" Then I added, "If you think you can, then you can. If you think you can't, then you can't. Go for it."

She gave an uncertain nod and started hobbling back to the track to do her final lap.

Her dad asked if he could help her, but I told him that if he assisted her now, then neither would know what she was capable of doing on her own.

"Cheer her on," I said, "but let her do this by herself."

The dad agreed, and the girl started walking. She was slow at first, with a little limp, but she kept on. The other kids cheered her on, but her dad cheered the loudest.

Before you knew it, her walk became a jog and then a run. She even sprinted the final few yards. She finished the race!

As each child crossed the finish line, one of the volunteers would put the medal around the child's neck. I handed the medal to her dad and said, "You need to be the one who puts this medal on her."

I wish I had a picture of their huge smiles at that moment. Both of them were winners. He was so incredibly proud of her, and she learned to never give up.

When it comes to dealing with trauma, there are no participation trophies. You get a medal when you finish.

That is why the recovery step is so important.

RECOVERY IS A CHOICE

After trauma, the obvious goal is to recover. In my experience, a lot of people are more afraid of this recovery step than they are of traumas and stresses.

Why? Because trauma and stress usually happen to us, are out of our control, and thrust upon us from the outside. Once they have happened, the act of recovery takes work and effort. It's a battle that comes at a mental, physical, and emotional cost.

At its core, recovery is a choice. That's where recovery begins. But once that choice is made, recovery is within reach.

Here are the four choices that accompany your recovery:

1. Choose hope (over despair).
2. Choose healing (over hurt).
3. Choose guilt (over shame).
4. Choose forgiveness (over condemnation).

These choices are the necessary parts of recovery. You get to "embrace" them because it's a choice that you make willingly. There is nobody controlling you.

And whether the trauma occurred long ago or the dust is still settling, this is where you reclaim control of your life.

No, the road to recovery does not always go smoothly, but it is gradual and in the right direction. Bouncing back and forth, successful one day, then struggling the next, that's all part of the ride. Don't beat yourself up about it.

 Now You Know:

You may see a door marked "fear and failure," but it is really the door to your freedom, and it always stands open.

Paul's words of encouragement always fit during recovery:

"For in due time we will reap if we do not grow weary" (Galatians 6:9 NASB).

It is your choice as to how and when you will emerge from your trauma experience. Choose to move forward out of your turmoil. Step by step, you will emerge victorious!

RECOVERY THROUGH HOPE

Recovery always starts with hope. Now, hope is not naïve optimism. It is not the giddy childlike expectation of Christmas morning. Nor is hope the denial of reality.

Hope is being fully aware of difficulties on the road to recovery, and yet moving ahead toward the inevitable light at the end of the tunnel. Hope is that spark, that little flame, that burns brightly in the darkness.

For some, their small spark of hope is the possibility that recovery might be possible. It's completely out of sight, but they move forward with hope that it exists. As American poet Theodore Roethke said, "Over every mountain there is a path, although it may not be seen from the valley."

 *Scripture Says:*

"As for me I will always have hope" (Psalm 71:14 NIV).

I like this verse. I'm sure Paul had it memorized.

Hope speaks the truth, "This will change. I will keep trying. I am worthy and worth it." But despair lies, "I'm not worth it. Nothing will work. There is no way out of this mess I'm in."

Trauma and PTSD often produce a persistent negative outlook on life, and that is marked by fear, shame, self-blame, and mistrust. This way of thinking never brings you up. It only takes you down.

But enough is enough!

There is always hope. So choose hope. And as small as that hope might be, it starts with imagining the possibility of possibilities. And from that tiny seed, it will grow.

Hope is even a little crazy. It sees good in tough times. That's why Paul would be happy that "suffering produces endurance, and endurance produces character, and character produces hope" (Romans 5:3–4 ESV). That's hope speaking.

Paul had a chance to practice hope when he was in the middle of a storm. The wooden cargo ship he was on was perhaps 180 feet long and probably carrying grain, along with 276 passengers. He was sailing in the Mediterranean Sea to Rome for his trial when they ran into a massive storm.

Even as the ship looked like it would surely sink, Paul did not lose hope. He encouraged the crew, the Roman soldiers, and the passengers to keep hope alive, assuring them that not a single life would be lost if they all remained on board. Hope calmed their panic and prevented foolish mistakes. Though their ship was smashed to pieces, Paul's hope endured, and everyone survived.

 Now You Know:

Hope is smart. It pushes you to stay motivated, choose healthy habits, and reject harmful temptations. All to your benefit!

A friend of mine, retired Vice Admiral Mike Miller, told me of a harrowing event when he commanded the aircraft carrier *USS John F Kennedy* during Hurricane Floyd in 1999. A mayday call came from a supply boat, the tug *Gulf Majesty*, which was foundering in the hurricane's high seas and winds.

With a flight deck that usually sits 60 feet above the water line, waves were actually crashing over the bow of that enormous ship. Knowing the risks, yet obligated to help other ships in distress, Miller ordered the carrier to turn toward the storm and the *Gulf Majesty* 140 miles away.

Meanwhile, the *Gulf Majesty* began to sink. Some of the crew managed to climb into an inflatable lifeboat, but it broke away before the rest of the crew could get aboard. The remaining crew jumped into the water, staying afloat with their life jackets and holding onto a broomstick, so they would not be separated from each other.

Helicopters from the *Kennedy* flew in gale force winds for more than an hour until they reached the location where the *Gulf*

Majesty had sunk. Then, despite 25-foot swells, they plucked the crew to safety.

The risks were not over, even when the helicopters returned, for they had to land on the carrier as it pitched up and down, side to side, fore and aft in the heavy seas. Thankfully, their skill and training were impeccable, and everyone landed safely.

Miller admits that it was a nail biting few hours from the time the helicopters took off until they returned. There were plenty of reasons to doubt, but Miller remained hopeful, and that lifted the determination and confidence of the crew.

Interestingly, an anchor is often used as a symbol of hope. And an anchor, which helps hold a ship in place during a storm, is only of value when it's under water and out of sight! That's when it does its job.

"We have this hope as an anchor for the soul, firm and secure" (Hebrews 6:19 NIV).

Hanging on to hope leaves no room for despair, and that's the point. Despair breeds depression, and that leads down the dead-end road of giving up. Despair is not a solution to any problem. It just makes things worse.

So the minute you start feeling despair trying to creep in, drop your anchor of hope! Drop it deep, and hang on to your hope. Hope is the fastest way to do a U-turn and get back in control.

RECOVERY THROUGH HEALING

Jesus asked a man who had been paralyzed for 38 years: "Do you want to get well?" The man responded with a series of complaints that no one would help him get into a pool of healing water. Jesus did not get detoured by the man's excuses, and instead told him to "get up" and walk and he did (John 5: 1–9).

As with hope, healing is a choice. However, this leads to a strange yet legitimate question:

Do you want to heal or do you want to hurt?

When I ask this question of my clients, many will hesitate before answering. They will say they definitely want to get better, but they want to negotiate the terms of their treatment.

What they are saying is this:

"I get to decide what work I will do."

What that means is this:

They will only do what they *want* to do, not what they *need* to do.

And how do you think that will work out for you?

"Do you want to stop the depression? Stop the anxiety?" I ask.

"Yes, of course," they all reply. Then some will add, "But do I really have to change my lifestyle? What I do? My beliefs?"

They want relief from the pain of depression and anxiety without actually addressing the source of the pain.

That's like putting a piece of black tape over the little warning light on your car dashboard. You won't see the bothersome red light anymore, but you didn't fix the problem, and that's dangerous!

Pain is a warning light that something is wrong. You can't fake it or cover it and expect to get better. It doesn't work that way.

To get to the source of the issue, to get the healing you really do want, is going to require you to take back control of your thoughts, feelings, and behavior.

That's first a choice. You must choose to heal.

Sure, it will take work, and you will probably hit a few bumps on your journey to healing, but you will get there. You will find the healing you want if you keep on going.

Believe it or not, some people actually resist healing. I've often wondered why that is the case, so over the years I collected a list of the obstacles that prevent people from healing from trauma. Here is the bullet version:

- **My constant grief honors their memory:** In trying to keep the memory of a lost loved one alive and not be disrespectful, we remain in a constant state of despair and get angry if anyone tries to talk us out of our depression.
- **I don't want to try because I don't want to fail again:** If we have tried to change before and repeatedly fallen short, healing is frightening. Each time we try and don't succeed, we conclude our case is more hopeless than we thought.
- **I don't want to get rid of my friends, because bad friends are better than no friends:** Toxic relationships, whether openly or passively, can make our life miserable every time we appear to gain strength. This is especially true when a narcissistic person holds us responsible for their happiness at the cost of our self-esteem.
- **Healing requires me to give up my vice:** Misery is a source of familiar comfort. We may not like it, but we are used to living with it. It's become our identity. Our trauma becomes a vice, like a drug, and we are convinced if we let go we will lose our sense of who we are.
- **Healing requires me to give up my anger and grudges:** Our trauma can lead to anger, and then fester into grudges that last an entire lifetime. We won't let it go, which means we will never heal.
- **Healing now proves I could have healed sooner, and I feel bad about that:** We fear if we can heal now, it means we were capable of doing so in the past, and we are then responsible for all the additional problems we caused over the years. To avoid guilt over the past, we prevent ourselves from healing in the present.

Now, before you discount this list as nonsensical, recognize that these obstacles are very real and make perfect sense to someone who is in the middle of the pain.

For example, I met a young man who visited the grave of fellow Marine every month. In the days leading up to and following each visit, he would get depressed. He explained, "I don't want to show up at the grave of my 'brother' all happy and stuff. He was blown apart, but his death also blew me apart. My sadness lets him know how much he meant to me."

That is no way to live, but to the young Marine, it made sense.

He eventually found healing by allowing himself to remember the good times they shared together. Now, as he visits the grave, he tells a funny story out loud about something the two of them did together. Maybe he will laugh, maybe he will cry, but he carries their friendship forward. Nobody is left behind or forgotten.

Eventually, he was able to understand this truth:

> Lost loved ones do not need or want us to be suffering. Those who truly love us did not want us to be miserable while they were alive, and certainly are not looking down from heaven wishing us eternal sadness. They want us to be happy, whole, and healed. And our family and friends who are still alive need us here and now, not buried in grief.

In another example, a client once told me, "I worked hard at getting better, and for the first time in my life I felt normal. But then I got scared, because I don't know how to do 'normal,' so I went back to all my problems again."

She never understood this fact:

> When our self-destructive behaviors, thoughts, or emotions erupt again, we must fight back anew. No ifs, buts, or excuses. It is totally up to us to decide if we are all in or out. Only one choice works, and that is healing.

I remember when my dad was in the depths of his alcoholism. I lost track of how many times he pledged to stop drinking, but he would return to the local bars saying, "I'm just going to go there to talk to friends; I'm not going to drink."

But that never worked. There was always some other person who said, "Oh, just have one" or "I don't want to drink alone" or "Are you too good for us?" My dad would always give in.

There was pressure on him from his friends to stay down. He couldn't break free until he realized that results wouldn't change if he didn't change. He had to put actual distance between himself and his "friends."

Thankfully, my dad learned this truth:

Those pressuring us to keep hurting are not our friends.
Let them go. Replace them with true friends who want us
to succeed.

Every obstacle that tries to keep you from healing has two sides, and you get to decide which side you want to live with.

PAUL WAS BETRAYED

Betrayal steals your trust, your heart, and your hope. It is a top source of emotional trauma. And you likely know the depth and breadth of this pain. Even worse is when those we supported in their times of greatest need are nowhere to be found during our time of need.

At his trial, Paul hoped someone who knew him would step forward and defend him, but that was not to be. The abandonment and alienation continued: "At my first defense, no one appeared on my behalf, but everyone deserted me" (2 Timothy 4:16 NASB).

It is hard to understand how others run away in the very moment when we feel like our existence hinges on their support, but they do. Some are frightened away by those who are struggling the most. Everyone wants a selfie picture with a star, but the same people flee from those who have fallen from grace. In this betrayal by abandonment, we feel unbearably and completely alone. This really, really hurts.

But rather than feel bitter, Paul did not get offended. He forgave, moved on, and remained faithful.

RECOVERY THROUGH GUILT

Like hope and healing, recovery through guilt is a choice. I know, this sounds confusing, but let me explain in the simplest of terms:

Guilt is *specific*, shame is *total*.

You see, one of the principal symptoms of PTSD is an exaggerated sense of blame against self or others. Shame crushes our souls.

Because guilt is specific, you can take responsibility for it. Guilt is also constructive, like constructive criticism. Guilt means "I *made* a mistake," and it is therefore in our power to heal psychological wounds.

On the other hand, shame means "I *am* a mistake, there is no chance of recovery." Shame is total, irreconcilable, and it saps your power to heal. Shame speeds up the downward spiral of destruction.

Paul knew the difference between guilt and shame. He pointed out:

"I now rejoice, not that you were made sorrowful, but that you were made sorrowful to the point of repentance" (1 Corinthians 7:9 NASB).

That is guilt at work, not shame.

The whole point of sorrow (feeling guilty for something) is repentance, from which you can turn and heal. Shame does not allow you to repent.

If you are truly guilty of something, then sorrow, regret, and remorse are appropriate feelings. You recognize you have wronged someone, accept responsibility for it, and look for ways to make amends.

In this way, guilt is good. It is the way to fix whatever has been broken.

Sadly, shame is usually what captures our attention. With it comes self-loathing, hatred, hopelessness, mental torment, and wrong behavior (quitting, isolation, and inflicting more hurt on ourselves). What's more, we reapply shame at regular intervals.

Shame is bad. It is also worthless, because it does not lead you to anything good, such as repentance or change.

I have seen people get caught up in the whirlwind of shame. They illogically believe their actions are unforgivable, declaring, "God made a mistake when He made me," with absolutely no chance to mend this broken vessel of our being. Fact is, we are not mistakes of creation.

Years ago, I was working with one of the many soldiers who served in Afghanistan and experienced the devastation of an improvised explosive device (IED) first hand. On that fateful day, he was the lead driver in a convoy, watching out for any signs of hidden bombs, so he could guide his convoy away from them. He missed seeing a buried IED and the vehicle behind his blew up. In it were several soldiers.

Amnesia and PTSD followed. He blamed himself for failing to see the hidden IED. He let shame drive him to isolation and depression. He took it another step further and decided he was therefore a failure as a husband.

Thankfully, his wife helped set him straight when she reminded him that her love was not based on perfection, and perfection was not required or expected anyway! "Do you remember our wedding vows?" she asked him. "We pledged our love in sickness and in health. There was nothing in there about being perfect."

Moving forward in the aftermath of trauma, blame can play tricks on you. If you were truly at fault, you should accept responsibility, but that does not apply to things outside of your control. Accepting justified personal responsibility will help keep you on the path to healing.

Clearly, shame is not guilt, but many people confuse the two. That should never be the case.

PAUL WAS FALSELY IMPRISONED

Paul was raised a Jew, and he believed Jesus to be the Messiah the Jews awaited. For Paul, it made perfect sense to preach this in synagogues. As he taught, he gained converts, and that threatened the Jewish leaders. He was questioned, threatened, and chased out of town repeatedly. On one occasion he was brought to trial, falsely accused, and imprisoned—chained to a wall—for two years.

False arrest, imprisonment and long delays in a fair trial can cause extraordinary psychological trauma. Paul's imprisonment was at the whim of the procrastinating governor. Unjust imprisonment has been known to cause hopelessness, aggression, suicidal thoughts, and lifelong damage. But Paul was not traumatized by it.

RECOVERY THROUGH FORGIVENESS

Like hope, healing, and guilt, recovery through forgiveness is also a choice. But forgiveness is something special because it is required. There is no way around it. The way to recovery is through forgiveness. And it comes down to this: God forgives; others might; I must.

It starts with embracing that no matter what we have done, *God forgives*. This will be extremely hard to accept if we are mired in shame. But it is true.

Others *might not* forgive you and remain in their anger and resentment. That hurts them and you. I cannot erase that pain affecting you, but we cannot let the absence of their forgiveness stop our own healing. "Love your enemies, do good to those who hate you" (Luke 6:27 NIV). Stop spending your time judging and being judged by others. You have enough work to do on your own.

Perhaps the hardest is being able to forgive ourselves for the harm we have caused, or the harm others have caused us.

You want healing and freedom ... it comes through forgiveness. Forgiveness does two amazingly powerful things:

#1—Forgiveness releases you from the grip of condemnation and all the hatred, bitterness, anger, revenge, grudges, resentment, vengeance, violence, gossip, and retribution that comes with it.

#2—Forgiveness replaces all the bad with empathy, compassion, love, understanding, kindness, grace, and reconciliation.

Thomas Aquinas wisely noted, "Anger is a passion for revenge that goes beyond the control of reason."

You don't want that!

You may not have had the power to stop the trauma at the time it happened, but you have the power to stop the trauma memory from hurting you right now. That is exactly what forgiveness does. It gives you back your power.

No, forgiveness does not change history, nor it does it erase what happened, or make it OK that it happened, but it does change how you react. And that is how it helps you break free from the grip of your trauma.

Irish author Oscar Wilde said it best: "Every saint has a past. Every sinner has a future."[1]

Your past is done. It's gone. What matters is your future.

Quite simply, forgive and move on . . . so your hurt from long ago has no authority over you today.

Take a minute to understand what forgiveness really is:

- Forgiveness is a choice. It cannot be bought or forced.
- Forgiveness is not hiding pain.
- Forgiveness is a commitment. Repeat "I forgive" as often as needed.
- Forgiveness is not conditional or partial.
- Forgiveness does not justify or condone harm.
- Forgiveness does not require you to be friends with the person who hurt you.
- Forgiveness is not forgetting or pretending things never happened.
- Forgiveness does not eliminate justice.
- Forgiveness is strength, power, courage, and love—not a sign of weakness in the slightest.

The reason you recover through forgiveness is:

1. Forgiveness releases you.
2. Forgiveness gives you command of your thoughts, feelings, and actions.
3. Forgiveness opens locked doors to your own learning.
4. Forgiveness relaxes in the acceptance that nobody, yourself included, is perfect.
5. Forgiveness resolves the cause of your pain, making hatred, anxiety, and depression no longer necessary.
6. Forgiveness removes the need for vengeance.
7. Forgiveness releases your stress.
8. Forgiveness reduces depression and anxiety, and gives you more hope.[2]

9. Forgiveness gives you strength.

Paul had much to say about forgiveness. Perhaps that is because of the forgiveness he received. Remember, he was guilty of persecuting and killing early Christians before he became such a strong defender of the faith. Knowing everything Paul did, God forgave him. So, whatever you did, God certainly can forgive you. And the fact is, God already has.

Paul wrote a lot about God's forgiveness, including:

> "In Him we have redemption through His blood, the forgiveness of our wrongdoings, according to the riches of His grace" (Ephesians 1:7 NASB).

> "God through Christ has forgiven you" (Ephesians 4:32 NLT).

> "He has delivered us from the domain of darkness and transferred us to the kingdom of his beloved Son, in whom we have redemption, the forgiveness of sins" (Colossians 1:13–14 ESV).

> "So if anyone is in Christ, there is a new creation: everything old has passed away; see, everything has become new" (2 Corinthians 5:17 NRSV).

God offers it. Not only should we accept it, but we should also offer it to others. It is not easy, but it is absolutely essential. Remember: God forgives. Others might. I must.

Recovery is always a choice, so keep moving forward with your recovery in each of these areas:

1. Your hope
2. Your healing

3. Your guilt
4. Your forgiveness

It's always the right choice.

 Scripture Says:

Isaiah 1:18; Psalm 51; Matthew 6:14; Matthew 18:21; Mark 11:25; Luke 15:11-32; Luke 17:3

Chapter 9

How to Apply Your Recovery

I knew a man who had a great-paying job. But he started to gamble his extra money, then his savings, and then his retirement funds. He also started drinking daily and spending less and less time at home, except to sleep off his hangover.

As you would expect, he lied to his wife about the money in their savings account and about his gambling and drinking problems. This created nonstop arguments at home, which he used as his excuse to spend even less time at home.

He told his wife that he would be away on a business trip for a few days, but she knew he was on a drinking and gambling junket. He came home to discover that his wife, their son, their furniture, and what little money was left in their bank accounts were gone. His wife left him a present, however: several thousand dollars more debt on his credit card.

Despondent over his financial losses, he worked more hours to keep himself busy and to pay the bills. Sleepless nights, exhaustion, and emotional pain caused him to make mistakes at work. He asked for a leave of absence, not realizing this meant he made himself ineligible for unemployment compensation.

No longer able to make payments on his mortgage, he lost his house. At that point, he was homeless, jobless, without his family, and in massive debt. His employer even refused to rehire him.

Feeling disgraced as a father, provider, husband, and man, and too embarrassed to ask for help, hopelessness and depression took over. He decided that he was too broken to fix. So he loaded his gun, put it in his mouth, and pulled the trigger.

Click.

It did not fire. "That single click scared the hell out of me," he told me later. "It was an alarm that woke me up out of my misery. There must be a reason I was spared. I decided to change my life instead of ending it."

His problems did not magically disappear, but he could take responsibility for his actions and work hard to repair, reconcile, and rebuild his life. That's what he did. Step by step, he built his life back.

YOU GET TO CHOOSE

Your recovery is rooted in your choice to embrace recovery with hope, healing, guilt, and forgiveness. These are powerful choices that lead directly to you walking in the freedom from your trauma that you want and deserve.

To practically apply each of these choices, you will want to:

1. **Repeat**: Make your choice a habit. It's not a single choice, but a decision to make repeatedly.
2. **Focus**: Think about what you want. Avoid movies, TV, people, or situations that feed misery and pessimism.
3. **Today**: Today is the day. Don't worry about yesterday or tomorrow.
4. **Ignore**: Don't worry about other people's lives. Your life is your focus.

5. **Dream**: Have goals and plans that motivate you to take action.
6. **Partner**: Always look for others to link arms with.
7. **Hang on**: You know what you want. You know where you are going. Endure. Persist. Press on.

As you embrace your recovery, each part will become easier, more natural, and second nature. Growth and freedom come as a direct result. It is inevitable!

HOW TO APPLY HOPE

Your recovery begins with hope. Paul knew the story of Job from the Old Testament and how Job lost his wealth, all of his livestock, his servants, and his children. Job was plagued by disease and immense suffering. Life could probably not have gotten much worse at that point, but Job somehow maintained his hope.

It was Job who said:

> "For there is hope for a tree, when it is cut down, that it will sprout again, and its shoots will not fail. Though its roots grow old in the ground and its stump dies in the dry soil, at the scent of water it will flourish and put forth sprigs like a plant" (Job 14:7–9 NASB).

Job would not be deterred. He kept a spark of hope alive. And in the end, Job got it all back, and then some!

In tough times, hope gives you strength and fortifies your courage. It keeps your head up as the waves of life crash over you.

It was Paul who wrote:

> "We are afflicted in every way, but not crushed; perplexed, but not despairing; persecuted, but not forsaken; struck down, but not destroyed" (2 Corinthians 4:8–9 ESV).

Through his own times of need, Paul's hope gave him the confidence to speak boldly and hold nothing back, even in the face of threats or when the confidence of others wavered.

Paul was unrelentingly hopeful, even when he had very little to back it up. That is a great example to all of us.

In addition to hope being a tool to help him recover from trauma, Paul's hope was also a source of joy. Paul challenged us: "Be joyful in hope" (Romans 12:12 NIV).

Hope is a choice, a constant choice, that you make and apply each and every day. So embrace hope. Let it carry you through any difficulties of your own recovery.

 *Scripture Says:*

Psalm 39; Psalm 71

HOW TO APPLY HEALING

Your recovery will include healing at many different levels. Some moments of healing will be small, some will be big, but every point of healing is a good one. Accept them all.

Paul is credited with many miracles, including touching handkerchiefs that were then placed on the sick, and they were healed (See Acts 19:11–12).

But healing others did not make Paul exempt from needing healing from his own trauma. Paul did not ask for pity nor did he complain, but he did cite his troubles to demonstrate how healing is possible despite massive physical and psychological trauma.

But what's interesting is that Paul doesn't describe healing as the absence or removal of suffering, but rather the state of being made better, stronger, or perfected.

PAUL TOOK CONTROL

To be transformed our destructive attitudes must be attacked head on. Paul said, ". . . the old things have passed away, behold new things have come" (2 Corinthians 5:17 NASB).

"Transform" requires us to be active in the process. As Paul said, the only way we can control our reckless beliefs is to take full control of those beliefs.

How? Through sharing our stories of trauma, we share the emotional weight. Soldiers swapped stories of tragedy and triumph around the campfire after battle. In the course of these conversations, what started as the property of a warrior became the property of the community at large. They encouraged each other, and suggested more effective ways to deal with problems. They learned to substitute feelings of helpless torment with emotions of hope, strength, and courage. This is how we practice making every thought captive.

Obviously, this is not about being perfect. Only God is perfect, and we as humans will always make mistakes. Instead, Paul is saying that when we give God our brokenness and ask for His help, God perfects us.

More accurately, He brings to an end, finishes, fully matures, and completes us so that we are whole. Basically, this is when you reach your full potential!

Paul wrote:

> "I don't mean to say that I have already achieved these things or that I have already reached perfection. But I press on to possess that perfection for which Christ Jesus first possessed me" (Philippians 3:12 NLT).

"That ye may stand perfect and complete in all the will of God" (Colossians 4:12 KJB).

You are to be the perfect versions of yourself. That is you, healed and whole. That is not a pressure call to be a Nobel Laureate, valedictorian, or hall of famer.

Instead, your job and my job is to complete the purpose for which we were made, flaws and all. To do this, we need to let go of whatever harms us or holds us back.

You get to choose healing rather than staying hurt. Here is what applying your healing looks like:

1. **Commit**: Healing requires you to make a commitment, not a bargain.
2. **Be patient**: Be persistent, for healing takes time.
3. **Support yourself**: Use your resilience and resistance tools to support yourself through recovery.
4. **Delete**: Get rid of the thoughts that define you by your diagnosis. For example, replace "I'm hurt and broken" with "I'm healing."
5. **Prune**: Get rid of unproductive and harmful thoughts, behaviors, or emotions. Don't hang on to anything you don't want.
6. **Press on**: Understand your healing is a process of becoming the best version of yourself. Never give up on that quest.

Oddly enough, I have met some people who want to stop the pain without really healing. I have heard such questions as, "Can I stop my addiction and still use heroin?" and "Can I not feel lonely and still hate myself?" and "Can I keep my toxic relationships and not be abused?"

No, you cannot simultaneously stay broken and get healed. It doesn't work that way. It can't work that way. You must let go of the hurt in order to be healed.

Healing comes when you choose it.

HOW TO APPLY GUILT

After applying hope and healing, your recovery moves to the often confused but vitally important step of guilt. With trauma, blame must be addressed, and the way to effectively deal with blame is with guilt rather than with shame.

Shame only breaks us, like a jackhammer to the soul. I have seen people interpret trauma as punishment for their sins or they feel dirty, damaged, and worthless because of it. Those are the characteristics of shame. It squishes life, but it's not reality.

 Now You Know:

Anything keeping you from acknowledging your honest responsibility is not going to heal you.

Reject shame by accepting guilt, but ONLY if you are truly responsible for what happened.

Just as you cannot blame others for your own decisions or actions, so you cannot blame yourself or accept blame for something that was out of your control. This blaming is not only a waste of time and energy, it enables evil, bad people, lies, anxiety, and fears to run rampant.

The answer is genuine, honest, and humble responsibility. That is what guides our path to a strong recovery.

A Marine General summed it up perfectly when he gave me this advice: "You mess up. You fess up. Now get up!"

That's it! Nothing more and nothing less.

There is a powerful story in the Bible of guilt, shame, and responsibility. It's the story of King David, Bathsheba, and her husband, Uriah. Here's a quick summary:

Uriah was off fighting in battle, while King David stayed home instead of assuming his rightful role as leader of his troops. David's lustful attraction to Bathsheba led to her pregnancy. Both she and David could have been killed for adultery, so David tried to cover it up by calling Uriah back from war, hoping Uriah would sleep with Bathsheba and then all would assume Uriah was the father. But Uriah felt it was wrong to be with his wife while his soldiers were fighting, so he spent the night sleeping outside David's door. What a loyal man! When Uriah returned to the battle, David had Uriah assigned to the front line where he would be killed, and he was (2 Samuel 11).

To make the betrayal even worse, Uriah had been one of King David's closest friends, one of his "mighty men" who helped David rise to power.

All told, David's list of transgressions included lust, adultery, cowardice, lies, a coverup, murder, betrayal, ignoring God, and trying to outrun his own guilt.

David was eventually confronted with his string of sins and was forced to face punishment. At that point, when facing his own guilt and desiring to reconcile with God, David repented. Here is a record of his admission of guilt, remorse, and plea for mercy:

> Have mercy on me, O God,
>   according to your steadfast love;
> according to your abundant mercy
>   blot out my transgressions.
> Wash me thoroughly from my iniquity,
>   and cleanse me from my sin.
> For I know my transgressions,
>   and my sin is ever before me.
> Against you, you alone, have I sinned,
>   and done what is evil in your sight,

so that you are justified in your sentence
and blameless when you pass judgment
(Psalm 51:1–5 NRSV).

Only when David accepted responsibility and guilt could he begin the process of rebuilding his life. David messed up big time, but he recovered. So, too, when we face up to our own transgressions, no matter how big, we can restart or rebuild.

What's incredible is that God did not abandon David after all of this! The Lord said David was a "man after my own heart" (1 Samuel 13:14), continued to work in and through David, and from the line of David's descendants came Jesus.

Besides David, there were dozens of other prominent figures in the Bible, including Paul, who shared a common background of failure and sin, yet none of them was condemned to shame. For each of them, guilt was a powerful teaching tool, fortifying their commitment and dedication to living life to its fullest.

PAUL TOOK RESPONSIBILITY

Paul admitted his guilt over the deadly persecutions against early Christians. He took full responsibility and accepted the consequences.

He also called on others to be responsible for themselves, writing: "For each one should bear their own load" (Galatians 6:5).

Armed with hope and a commitment to healing, the steps to unlocking your recovery with guilt are pretty simple:

1. Acknowledge your mistakes.
2. Take responsibility.
3. Accept deserved guilt.

And then you move forward!

HOW TO APPLY FORGIVENESS

Applying guilt to hope and healing leads your recovery efforts right up to the point of breakthrough. The way to cross over is through the act of forgiveness. And forgiveness, as you know, is always a choice.

Holding on to unforgiveness is also a choice, but it's not a smart one. Those who never let go and refuse to forgive will end up:

- **Fighting when there is no need**: Consumed with anger and retaliation, they remain revved up for a fight. Their minds obsess with replaying ugly memories and plotting revenge. They have a short temper, little tolerance for the mistakes of others, and no room for empathy.
- **Having trouble feeling loved**: Filled with self-condemnation, they cannot accept love from others. They think they should be punished and are not worthy of love.
- **Projecting negative emotions onto others**: Their internal condemnation leads them to distrust everyone and reject all emotional support, both giving as well as receiving. They hold back love, expect perfection, and are easily disappointed.
- **Hating themselves**: They can't stop self-loathing and self-punishing and even think of suicide because they won't forgive themselves.
- **Infecting others**: Children raised in an atmosphere of coldness and emotional distance, all part of an unforgiving environment, will tend to repeat what they have learned.
- **Being forever vulnerable**: By never fixing the problem, they remain weak, vulnerable, and easily susceptible to temptations to continue hiding the issue.

Clearly, letting go through forgiveness is a good, smart, healthy decision. To truly free ourselves from the pains of the past and allow ourselves to change, we need to forgive.

Forgiveness is a choice. I say "I must" as my own commitment. You have to make your own commitment. Nobody can control you. Coercion and peer pressure have no say in the matter. It's totally up to you.

But if you do want to heal, to be healthy and whole, to achieve the recovery you want . . . you need to be able to say, "I forgive."

Yes, this is often hard, especially when it comes to forgiving the people who never change, such as the bossy in-law, the bullying husband, the nagging wife, the selfish daughter, the deceitful son, all who steal, all who betray, and so many more.

How is it possible to forgive them? Only, I think, by remembering that I am constantly asking God to forgive me. And if I'm not willing to forgive others, I can't expect God to forgive me.

Forgiveness is supposed to go both ways:

> If you forgive people their sins, your Father in heaven will forgive your sins also. If you do not forgive people their sins, your Father will not forgive your sins (Matthew 6:14–15 NLV).

Paul said it this way:

> Let all bitterness and wrath and anger and clamor and slander be put away from you, along with all malice. Be kind to one another, tenderhearted, forgiving one another, as God in Christ forgave you (Ephesians 4:31–32 ESV).

Forgiving yourself or forgiving others does not absolve anyone of responsibility, and life isn't all unicorns and rainbows after that, but it does allow you to change and recover. It breaks you out of the rut of blame and shame. It frees you to think and feel in a new way!

Paul was a master at forgiveness. He forgave himself for all the persecutions, including torture and killings, by his own hands.

That's pretty intense! But he knew that unless he could forgive himself and accept God's forgiveness, he could not carry on his work. Paul practiced what he preached: "forgiving each other; as the Lord has forgiven you, so you also must forgive" (Colossians 3:13 ESV).

 Now You Know:

We need to forgive the inexcusable because God has forgiven the inexcusable in us.

But this is where some people get stuck. So let me ask you:

Is there something you have done that God doesn't know about? No, because God knows everything.

Is there something you have done that is so bad that God would not and could not forgive you? No, because God freely forgives anyone and everyone who asks for forgiveness.

Is there a valid reason then why you have not forgiven yourself? No, there isn't. So let it go! Choose to forgive yourself. If God forgives you, and He does, then you can certainly forgive yourself.

It's easier to accept God's forgiveness when we understand His love toward us. His love is unconditional, active, unselfish, open, deep, obedient, loyal, and never ending.

Those are nice words, but God also backed it up with action. Paul nailed it when he wrote these words:

But God demonstrates his own love for us in this: while we were still sinners, Christ died for us (Romans 5:8 NIV).

At our worst, in our dirtiest moment, when we had no thought of asking for forgiveness . . . *that* is the moment when Jesus willingly went to the cross for us. For you.

Now THAT is love.

So don't think for a moment that God can't love you or won't forgive you. That's a total lie. Don't block His love. Let it in. Accept His forgiveness and forgive yourself.

That is how lives are transformed.

Keep on receiving His forgiveness, because He keeps on giving it. He wants you to be whole, and forgiveness is right there any time you need it.

Then comes forgiving others.

Paul chose to forgive those who hurt him. He did not let their attacks sideline him in that moment or later in the future. He didn't dwell on it. Instead, he let it go and went right on with his work.

When you forgive others, you pull out their poisoned words, deeds, or actions and cover the wounds with love. That is how you walk free.

Here are seven steps to getting and giving forgiveness:

Step #1—Admit and accept responsibility. This breaks the power of shame, and allows guilt to work.

Step #2—Say it aloud to someone. This brings it into the light so you can see it and work on it.

Step #3—Be honest and specific. This is open, real, clear, humble, and complete.

Step #4—Be sorry, with humility. This is true regret for your actions.

Step #5—Pay your dues. This is you fixing what you broke and making amends with those you hurt.

Step #6—Commit to change. This is you actually changing and being transformed (having a change of heart, mind, and actions).

Step #7—Reconcile. This is, to the best of your ability, putting the pieces back together after the trauma.

That final part of forgiveness is reconciliation. Usually, reconciliation is a two-way street in that it involves both parties, but sometimes it can only be accomplished by one of the people involved. That's fine, it still works, but ideally reconciliation includes those involved. That is because reconciliation restores lives and relationships.

This is what reconciliation is:

> It is a declaration that no matter what someone did to you (or what you did to that someone), you will no longer carry the burden of the trauma.

As you know, this does not erase history. Instead, you are transforming your thoughts and emotions to reclaim who you were meant to be.

Had I forgiven my father and reconciled with him years earlier, I believe I could have avoided many of my own problems. By letting go, I would have been free. I thought by not forgiving him, I was repaying the hurt to him. Instead, I held on, and it only hurt me. Dumb.

Someone once said that unforgiveness is like drinking poison and then hoping the person who hurt you will die. Not a good idea!

 Now You Know:

Being sorry for getting caught, but not sorry for what you did, does not count as asking for forgiveness.

You cannot change the fact that trauma has brought you to this point, but you can change what you are doing now, and you can change where you are going in the future.

Maybe you heard a while back about a shooting by a police, where Officer Amber Guyer was found guilty of killing Botham Jean. Did you know that Botham's brother, Brandt, spoke up in the courtroom and forgave of his brother's killer? He even asked the judge, "I don't know if this is possible, but can I give her a hug, please?" As the two embraced, the sounds of sobbing filled the courtroom.

But something else happened for Brandt. His act of forgiveness and reconciliation set him free! No doubt Amber was impacted as well, but it was Brandt who purposefully did what it took to get free. For him, it was an act of reconciliation.

A friend of mine, Barry Werber, gave me permission to tell this story of his own brave act of reconciliation. Barry was 76 when a gunman attacked his synagogue in Pittsburgh on the morning of Saturday, October 27, 2018.

When the shots were fired, Barry ran into the storage closet right off their sanctuary with two other members. Eleven died that day in the deadliest anti-Semitic attack in US history to date.

In the months that followed, Barry wrestled with horrible memories of the scenes. He has asked himself hundreds of times how the shooter could not see him in that closet? Why was he spared, while others died?

In April 2019, Barry, his wife Brenda, and I went back to visit the synagogue. The security guard opened the gate of the wire mesh fence that still surrounded the building. Broken windows were boarded up with plywood. Inside, the rooms were left exactly as they were on the day of the shooting in order to preserve evidence. The exception was the large holes cut out of the walls. Following Jewish tradition, anything stained with the blood of a victim had been removed and buried in the cemetery. On a table lay a prayer book with a bullet hole.

As we approached a set of stairs, the guard asked Barry if he wanted to take the elevator. But Barry said his friend Cecil Rosenthal died on those stairs, and if he did not go down them now, he never would. We walked down those steps then turned toward the sanctuary door on the right. In solemn reverence, we entered. Every one of Barry's movements was in slow motion, his eyes constantly scanning the room. Chairs were randomly scattered about. The Torah was out and not in the Ark where it otherwise would be placed except during a service. The Ner tamid (eternal light) was still glowing. Barry walked to a lectern in the middle of the room. There he placed a photo he had taken years before, of his friends processing with their Torah to their new home at Tree of Life. All three were killed in the shooting. Barry paused in silence for several moments. Then he said aloud a prayer in Hebrew and English. *"Barukh atah Adonai eloheinu melekh ha-olam . . .* Blessed art Thou, oh Lord our God, King of the Universe, who has allowed us to gather to mourn those that we have lost."

Afterward, he reflected on what helped him return. He recalled hearing a nurse who was wounded that day say, "You have to face your fears or they rule you." And Barry added, "I did not want the shooter to have any control over me. It was sad, but it didn't hurt me. I am done. I'm no longer controlled."

Barry leaves it to the courts and God to administer justice to the man responsible for this carnage. Barry admits forgiveness is very difficult for him, but finds comfort in being able to use his own power for the purpose of good. His last memories of those rooms are no longer about that awful day in October 2018, but of a new day in April 2019. He reclaimed the synagogue as a place for worship, he reclaimed the rooms to be filled with the blessed memories of dear friends, and he reclaimed control of his own life. It was a reconciliation in his own heart and spirit.

The act of reconciliation looks different for everyone. I have known war veterans to revisit battlefields or meet with their former enemies. I know of adults who lay wreaths at the graves of their abusive parents, and women who place flowers at the locations where they were hurt. Many write notes detailing their pain, then burn them or throw them into the sea.

Whatever your approach, the point is to get free! And whether it's physical or mental, when you return to places where you were powerless in your past, you reclaim control of your future.

Chapter 10

Step #4—Accept Your Renewal

Over a period of two years, Leah's life was turned upside down. First, their car was totaled in an accident, but thankfully nobody was hurt.

Then they took their retirement fund and invested it in their family business, only to see it fail completely. They had to file for bankruptcy and were forced to close their doors. In the end, after 20 years in business, they had nothing, zero, no assets at all.

Then one evening while they were home, a kitchen stove fire quickly spread through the house, destroying nearly everything they had. Leah's husband did manage to pull the car out of the garage, but the family watched everything else go up in flames.

The Red Cross put the family up in a local motel and members of their church donated used clothes. Leah tried to keep her children's lives as normal as possible, so two days later she drove them to school.

Driving back to the motel, she broke down in tears. Her heart felt overwhelmed, and she was bombarded with fears. "Could things get any worse?" she wondered.

At an intersection, as she waited for the light, a funeral procession came through. She watched the lead car carrying the casket, the next car with the grieving family, and then the many other cars of family and friends that followed.

In that moment, she realized that everyone in her own family was alive and healthy. Her despair over her losses was suddenly transformed into gratitude. Her family was safe!

From somewhere deep within, she felt unexpected joy. She knew that her family would make it. Yes, they would need to rebuild, but they could do it! It would be a fresh start, but they would do it together.

That moment was a turning point for her. It was the shift when she went from surviving to thriving.

RENEWAL IS A CHOICE

What exactly is renewal? What does it mean? How is it a step toward freedom from trauma?

These are great questions. I'll use Paul to explain it. He wrote:

> So we do not lose heart. Though our outer self is wasting away, our inner self is being *renewed* day by day. For this light momentary affliction is preparing for us an eternal weight of glory beyond all comparison, as we look not to the things that are seen but to the things that are unseen. For the things that are seen are transient, but the things that are unseen are eternal (2 Corinthians 4:16–18 ESV).

As we've wondered and asked already, why didn't Paul have debilitating PTSD as a result of all his trauma?

It was in part because he let all the previous steps (resilience, resistance, and recovery) lead him up to this point, and then he accepted renewal. Acceptance is not passive. It is a transformative surrender to the restorative power of renewal.

Paul was quick to tell his *not-so-secret secret* of what renewal is made of: faith, trust, grace, and a mission. He specifically said,

"I have learned the secret . . ." and that secret is Christ's cure: "I can do all things through Him (Christ) who strengthens me" (Philippians 4:12,13 NKJB, NASB).

With renewal:

- You are no longer just surviving.
- You no longer need to deny, despair, or fight anxieties and worries.
- You are free to fully and completely release old ways.
- You are reborn, unafraid, unrestrained, and transformed by a renewing of your mind.

It is time to move on.

Paul echoed this truth when he stated:

"When I was a child, I talked like a child, I thought like a child, I reasoned like a child. When I became a man, I put the ways of childhood behind me" (1 Corinthians 13:11 NIV).

This will all make more sense as you take the step of accepting your renewal. Here are the four choices that accompany your renewal:

1. Choose faith (over doubt).
2. Choose trust (over mistrust).
3. Choose grace (over emptiness).
4. Choose a mission (over wandering).

These choices are the necessary parts of your renewal.

RENEWAL THROUGH FAITH

The word "faith" is more than just confidence we have in someone or something.

Faith is the assurance of things hoped for, the conviction of things not seen (Hebrews 11:1 ESV).

The faith fueling our renewal is faith in God—that He is trust-worthy, good, able and willing to help, bigger than any of our problems. The offer is on the table. Whether or not we accept it makes the difference.

Renewal begins with faith. When our focus is on our faith in God, we are transformed from the inside out.

Faith is a belief that is accompanied by supportive behaviors, emotions, and actions. It's not all head knowledge. Rather, it's head, heart, body, and spirit, all working together.

Faith requires action. That's true faith. James, who worked and traveled with Paul, explained it well:

> But someone will say, "You have faith; I have deeds."
> Show me your faith without deeds, and I will show you
> my faith by my deeds (James 2:18 NIV).

I have had people ask me at this point, "Wait! Hold on. Can't I get healed from my trauma without faith in God?"

That's a good question, but I have witnessed this reality hundreds and hundreds of times:

> Full recovery from trauma never ends, is never fully satis-fied, with only earthly pleasures and rewards.

There is a spiritual element to freedom and healing from trauma that cannot be ignored. Faith is not a temporary fill to an eternal void. Rather, it is an answer to an inner desire, inner yearning, an inner calling that can only be satisfied in one way. People care, but Christ cures.

Some have called this the "God-sized hole in our hearts." Like a puzzle piece that only fits exactly in one place, so too the hole in our heart is only filled with a faith in God.

Blaise Paschal in 1699 described this hole inside of each one of us:

> What else does this craving, and this helplessness, pro-claim but that there was once in man a true happiness, of

which all that now remains is the empty print and trace? This he tries in vain to fill with everything around him, seeking in things that are not there the help he cannot find in those that are, though none can help, since this infinite abyss can only be filled with an infinite and immutable object; in other words, by God himself.[1]

But if we refuse faith, we are choosing to stifle our own healing. That is because the old unproductive paths to escape—attacking ourselves with doubt and despair, distracting ourselves with more work, jumping through multiple relationships, lusting for more power, or drowning it with substance abuse—are not answers.

 Now You Know:

When you endure the worst of times, you become better because of it.

Faith cannot be avoided, especially in regards to healing from trauma. I tell people, "Accept it, so you can fully and fundamentally be transformed."

What about doubts and questions? Go ahead, ask away, but don't let that slow you down from moving forward. Why not? Because you may not get an answer right away, if at all.

Now, don't let that offend you. Isn't it a little strange that we humans demand that God, the creator of the entire universe, who knows all things, and who lives outside of time, answer *our* questions immediately and on our terms?

If He doesn't, we claim He doesn't exist or doesn't love us.

I'm sorry, but that is completely illogical! I mean, do we really have the right to ask the questions on this test of our faith? When taking any test in school, it's the teachers who ask the questions, not the students.

Faith is not about being in control. Rather, faith is letting go, and being OK with that.

Faith really does help us heal from trauma and stress. Many studies have proven that. One study by Baetz and Bowen[2] reviewed the records of 37,000 adults regarding reported pain from fibromyalgia, back pain, migraine headaches, and chronic fatigue syndrome. Those who identified themselves as "spiritual" but not "religious" (regular attendance at worship services) were more likely to have these conditions, while those who practiced a religion using prayer to cope with their chronic conditions were more likely to have better psychological health.

Veterans with higher spirituality/religiosity tended to cope better with their PTSD and are less likely to be involved with substance abuse and risk-taking behaviors, and they reported better moods.[3] Those with lower spirituality/religiosity had lower recovery rates from PTSD.[4]

For many with PTSD, spiritual issues are fundamental to healing. Moral injury (MI) in trauma is much easier to treat when discussions include faith. MI is defined as "perpetrating, failing to prevent, bearing witness to, or learning about acts that transgress deeply held moral beliefs,"[5] marked by symptoms of shame, self-condemnation, and deep moral struggles. Unresolved concerns about MI can be a barrier to healing.

Unfortunately, many counselors and mental health professionals do not address the role of faith in healing, and as a result, they are missing an opportunity to help those in need. Some try so hard to be politically correct by not talking of faith that they end up being politically incorrect by not talking about faith. Their clients assume it must be a taboo subject if their therapist won't talk about it.

The fact is, faith is an essential part of renewal.

When I worked as a psychologist in the Navy, even military service members who defined themselves as "agnostic" found faith to be a tremendous help in their healing. Those who kept their memories of battle horrors alive often maintained their anger, alcoholism, and self-loathing. Many said that their search for a new direction in their lives was enhanced when they accepted faith in their lives.

Novelist Agatha Christie nailed it when she wrote in her book, *Appointment With Death*: "There is nothing in the world so damaged that it cannot be repaired by the hand of almighty God. I encourage you to know this because without this certainty we should all of us be mad."

Suppose you agree that faith is a necessary part of healing from trauma. How do you go about building your faith?

A strong faith is built by first choosing it, then by walking in humility, and then grown with persistent prayer.

 Now You Know:

When trust is broken, relationships with other people are more vulnerable.

Paul's advice makes sense:

Pray without ceasing (1 Thessalonians 5:17 ESV).

God is always right beside you, ready to help you heal from your trauma. Open your eyes and heart so you can experience the full comfort that faith provides.

That is faith in action.

RENEWAL THROUGH TRUST

On the journey of healing from trauma, right behind faith is trust. They go hand in hand. Think of it this way:

- Faith is believing God exists; trust is *knowing* He will act.
- Faith is a relationship with God; trust is complete confidence and reliance on Him.

- Faith welcomes God into our lives; trust perseveres through the difficulties of life.

As you would expect, a breakdown in trust is nearly universal with trauma. It then follows that re-establishing trust is essential for renewal.

And thankfully, trust can be restored. It will take time and effort to fix trust that has been broken.

Don't let someone's negative "it's all in your head" comment discourage you, because broken trust does actually affect your brain and your whole body. From earlier chapters, you know that your brain works to protect you. It likes things to be safe and predictable, but trauma ruins that. Replaying the heartbreak of betrayal causes your brain to remain on hyper alert, and that affects your stress levels and overall health.

This is interesting:

> People who rate themselves as not trusting others also rate their own health as poor.[6]

By trying to protect you from further harm, your brain takes action to turn down your interest in activities, exercise, and relationships. Naturally, you trust people less, and that sets the stage for other issues, such as social avoidance, phobias, and panic attacks.

Strangely, your brain, in its desperate desire to get back to normal and stable, can also push you into harmful relationships. The "it feels good" is not true trust, just your brain being so hungry for trust that it fools you into making bad decisions.

This is called "trauma bonding," when people choose to stay connected with their abuser, even blaming themselves for their abuser's behavior, all because of a distorted version of trust as a result of their own trauma.

That's why trauma victims often say, "I don't know what is true anymore."

At that point:

- It's a lonely place to not trust others.
- It's a scary place to not trust the natural world.
- It's a painful place to not trust ourselves.
- It's a discouraging place to not trust God.

What can you do? Can you trust anyone ever again? Yes, but you should understand that disappointment is inevitable. I mean, do you always trust yourself? I don't always trust myself. I'm not perfect. We will make mistakes.

Pop culture wisdom says that you should "trust your heart," but that is nonsense. You know very well that trusting your fickle feelings is not wise, safe, or smart. Feelings change in a second! And if your feelings are all over the place due to trauma, you should really be careful.

You need stability again. And that is where trust comes in. Your trust needs to be anchored on something solid, so that your heart, mind, body, and soul can breathe again. You need to regain your footing.

What's the answer?

Quite simply, it's trusting God. That will be different for each person and different at every step of the journey, but God is the ultimate healer, counselor, and lover of your soul. He wants you healthy and whole.

That's partly why we are told:

> Trust in the Lord with all your heart and do not lean on your own understanding (Proverbs 3:5 ESV).

Paul knew those words by heart, and he lived them.

A friend of mine learned this truth in a very real way. One day he was driving home when he saw smoke in the distance. It was his own house, on fire, with smoke pouring out of the windows.

"Is everyone out?" he yelled, as he jumped out of his car.

When he heard that his son and niece were still inside, probably upstairs in their bedrooms, he climbed up the porch roof and into the second-story window. On his hands and knees, feeling the scorching heat on the floor, he crawled down the smokey hallway toward his son's bedroom.

Inside, he found his unconscious son in bed, and immediately carried him out the window to safety.

He went back in again to find his niece. The fire was spreading. Unable to see through the opaque smoke, he became disoriented, but he calmed himself and navigated by touch.

Eventually, he got to the room where she was sleeping. Staying low to the floor, he reached up onto her bed and found her. Cradling her unconscious body, he carried her out.

Afterward he said, "I knew if I went in, I might not live, but I also knew if I did not go in, I would not want to live. So, I had to trust God would guide me to find her."

Through trust, He gave sight where my friend had none. Trust made all the difference in bringing him courage, endurance, persistence, and hope when he needed it the most.

And you need it too when you are fighting, walking, or crawling your way forward, past your trauma, toward health and healing. Put your trust in Him.

Concerned that your trust in God might be misplaced? That maybe God doesn't know you or your situation well enough to take care of you? Paul wrote:

> The foolishness of God is wiser than men, and the weakness of God is stronger than men (1 Corinthians 1:25 ASV).

You can trust God.

Paul humbly accepted the reality (as should we) that he did not have the wisdom or strength to handle everything in life. Paul surrendered his anxieties to God, which gave him freedom. He didn't need to carry emotional burdens all by himself. He could trust God with all of it.

And so can you.

PAUL WAS TORTURED

Torture can cause extensive psychological damage to the victim. Often, victims of torture experience long-lasting anxiety, shame, rage, and expressions of violence toward others.

The rage is not just directed at the perpetrators, but can be expanded even to loved ones. Family and friends are also profoundly affected, as they witness the victim's pain and subsequent effects.

Paul's torture should have left him emotionally isolated and angry, but it didn't.

RENEWAL THROUGH GRACE

Very early one summer morning, I was out for a run with a friend who had retired after serving 25 years in military special forces. Usually, he never spoke about his combat experiences, but that morning he said, "There's an ugly scene that keeps jumping back into my mind lately."

As we jogged down the bike path, he told me some of the details, and I could understand why it bothered him!

After a long pause, I asked, "You OK?"

He exhaled deeply, shook his head as if he were shaking water from his hair, and replied, "Fine, fine. I'm good. I'm good."

Then, after a few more quiet minutes, he went on to tell me how his uncle served in Vietnam, and when he returned, he never got married, never had kids, and pretty much kept to himself.

"He didn't talk much or show much feeling," my friend added. "I vowed I'd never handle the s—t like he did. I've got grace on my side, and that keeps me strong."

Looking back at his words, I realize my friend said three very profound things that day:

1. Flashbacks can still occur years after the trauma.
2. Some people stop scary feelings by stopping all feelings.
3. Accepting grace enables us to overcome, not just tolerate, our torments. We can safely love again.

His uncle probably suffered from anhedonia, which is where we are unable to feel pleasure. We lose empathy and then emotionally isolate ourselves. We may not even care that we do not care. All of these are common symptoms when suffering from PTSD and depression.

Behind the pain is a heart that wants to love and be loved, a heart that wants to feel empathy and connect with people, a heart that wants to trust again. The desire is there, but the trauma has covered it, like a thick shell around the heart.

Think of where you are:

- You have come so far!
- You can look back over your progress and know the times of your troubles are behind you.
- You are not your trauma.
- You are not your disease.
- You are not your stress.
- You are not the negative label others have placed on you.
- You certainly are not the shameful label you painted on yourself.
- You are healing with more strength and courage and hope than you first thought you had in you!

Of course, flashbacks and doubt may resurface from time to time, but this does not mean you have failed. Not in the slightest.

No evil has the right to grab ownership of your heart again. Paul said this battle for the heart was the most important battle to fight. Here is the truth that Paul would tell you:

Are you worthy of being loved? YES!
Are you able to love again? YES!
Will you find this love anywhere? YES!

My special forces friend understood depression and PTSD, and he saw where it led his uncle. He also knew it was possible to live again. The answer, he found, was grace.

That is exactly what Paul was saying when he wrote:

But he said to me, "My grace is sufficient for you, for my power is made perfect in weakness" (2 Corinthians 12:9 NIV).

Despite his intense faith, Paul was still burdened by internal battles that left him feeling weak. He identified "grace" as what carried him through his personal torments.

Paul also said this about the grace he received:

For I am the least of the apostles, who am not fit to be called an apostle, because I persecuted the church of God. But by the grace of God I am what I am, and His grace toward me did not prove vain; but I labored even more than all of them, yet not I, but the grace of God with me (1 Corinthians 15: 9-10 NASB).

What is this grace that Paul and my friend were talking about? Here is what I believe grace is:

#1—Grace is unmerited love. If something is "merited," then it's due you, such as wages or rights as a citizen. But grace is unmerited. You simply can't earn it. Grace is freely given. Thankfully, perfection is not required. In fact, grace is the perfect given to the imperfect.

Some say grace is undeserved, but I disagree. You see, parents love their child because that child is *their* child. The child needs to do nothing to receive the parents' love, but the child deserves the parents' love. That's what parents are supposed to do: love, care, nourish, etc. In the same way, you were created, given life, and even thought about before you were born. You are not just a random blob of molecules. You are important to God, and because He made you, you deserve all that He offers, including His love, mercy, and grace.

You are worthy of and deserve His grace. What's more, He wants to give it to you. All you have to do is accept it.

#2—Grace is unending love. I once had a travel coupon for a free flight on an airline. By the time I decided to use it, I discovered the coupon had an expiration date. Grace is different. It has no expiration date. What's more, it's not something you can lose.

Like God's unconditional love toward you, grace is unconditional. Our human flaws may remain forever, yet the love through grace never runs out, and it never runs away. Like the parent who loves their child despite the child's crippling addiction, arrests, or jail. The love endures.

Our shame, isolation, and condemnation may mask the grace that is freely given, but not seeing something is not proof that it doesn't exist. Grace is always there, patiently waiting, ready to guide you back home.

#3—Grace is unlimited love. Grace is big! Someone once explained that faith is our belief in God, and grace is God's belief in us. That is a humbling thought, for unlimited grace could only come from unlimited love.

Paul recognized that fact: "And that you, being rooted and grounded in love, may be able to comprehend with all the saints what is the breadth and length and height and depth, and to know the love of Christ which surpasses knowledge, that you may be filled up to all the fullness of God" (Ephesians 3:17–19 NASB).

#4—Grace completes us. If we are broken, shattered by trauma, and hurting, we are also probably not thinking that God wants to connect with us to help us heal. But God's grace is there to do just that—to put us back together! His grace completes us.

No matter the thoughts, feelings, symptoms, or results from trauma, grace can fill the holes. Grace can fix what's broken. Grace can rescue you. Grace restores a broken spirit. Grace completes you.

Years ago, I had the privilege of being on site when a family received the keys to their new home, thanks to Habitat for Humanity and the many volunteers who gave their time. After the ceremony, I walked around the yard to look over the house.

A seven-year-old boy was there, playing in the yard. I struck up a conversation, and he told me with the biggest smile that the new house was his house!

In that moment, I knew what grace was. He was just a kid, not responsible in any way for the financial situation his family was in. Nor was he able to build the house he now had. All of it, from beginning to end, from cause to completion, was beyond his control.

That's grace. It's simply a gift.

Paul knew that as well. He wrote:

> For it is by grace you have been saved, through faith—and this is not from yourselves, it is the gift of God (Ephesians 2:8 NIV).

RENEWAL THROUGH A MISSION

It was Winston Churchill who said, "It is not enough to have lived. We should be determined to live for something."

The last part of renewal is deciding on a purposeful mission. Your experiences have not just brought you to this point, they are finished chapters. The book of your own life is not fully written.

I urge you to live with purpose, to choose a mission, to make a difference, and to use all that you have been through to help others. A mission is always better than wandering.

It is often said that your job is how you make *money*, but your mission is how you make a *difference*. You worked hard on your healing and took control of your trauma. What you learned has enormous value when you teach others what you have learned.

If I may be so bold:

> You are called to a mission that serves others, to give them hope and to mentor by example, word, and deed.

What you have gathered through your own renewal is not yours to keep any more than a harvest of seeds should remain in the barn. Sow into the lives of others.

That is because the pain and hurt you have experienced have been felt by countless others. It's always that way. You are never the only one.

James Hatch, a Navy SEAL who retired after 25 years in the Navy, flew 150 combat missions before he was wounded and was pulled out. On his road to recovery, he trudged through months of rage, despair, depression, alcoholism, and suicidal thoughts. In his book *Touching the Dragon*, he penned these insightful words: "The deep-down soul medicine—the true healing—comes when you stop focusing on yourself and switch to helping others."

Kay Warren, who cofounded Saddleback Church in California with her husband, Rick, visited me in my office once. We talked about their son, Matthew, who fought depression for years and sadly took his own life at the age of 27 on April 5, 2013. She humbly admitted the sobering impact, pain, and doubt in her own life. But she did not quit. Her pain fueled her new calling, and that is to help meet the unmet needs of those suffering from depression. There are almost 50,000 suicides in the United States each year! People need to hear depression is real, and it is treatable. She is on a mission to help those in need.

Daryl Scott is the father of one of the students killed at Columbine High School. He now devotes all his time to sharing the story of his daughter, Rachel. I attended one of his talks, where he read several of her diary entries, often containing themes of her faith, her letters to God, and her compassionate observations of life. In one entry from May 1998, she wrote, "This will be the last year of my life, Lord. I have gotten what I can. Thank you." A year later, one of the Columbine shooters confronted Rachel outside the school and asked her, "Do you still believe in God?" as he pointed a gun at her head. Another student who was wounded near her recalled her answer: "You know I do." The shooter replied, "Then go be with him" as he pulled the trigger. To the end, Rachel stood courageously for her faith. For over 20 years, Daryl has continued to speak to students across the nation in his mission to have Rachel's life inspire respect and compassion.

Whatever your situation, look for ways to be of service to others. You have come too far to slide back or to just slide quietly away into the background. What's more, serving others actually helps you continue to heal and grow, because those who teach are the ones who learn the most.

Continue your everyday work. Don't stop. Often, there are daily opportunities to help others in need from your job or position. Some places of employment may even provide you with time or money to serve others in your area of expertise.

Scripture states:

> Each of you should use whatever gift you have received to serve others, as faithful stewards of God's grace in its various forms (1 Peter 4:10 NIV).

Whatever your talents and time availability, use them, give them, and share them. You don't have to start a big project or a new charity to make a difference. Just find something that allows you to continue to benefit others.

What you do is up to you. It is, after all, *your* mission.

❋ ❋ ❋

Renewal is always a choice, so keep moving forward with your renewal in each of these areas:

1. Your faith
2. Your trust
3. Your grace
4. Your mission

It's always the right choice.

Chapter 11

How to Apply Renewal

At a military hospital, I met with a soldier's wife about her husband's combat wounds, his progress, and prognosis. Months before, shrapnel had penetrated the left side of his head, inflicting a traumatic brain injury, leaving him with speech problems, changes in his personality, and significant paralysis on his right side.

Since the injury, he had relearned to walk, albeit awkwardly and requiring support. His speech came back partially, but it was still very difficult for him to pronounce words. He did not understand abstract language (such as metaphors), but he could carry on a basic conversation.

He still had no control of movements in his right hand and would need to relearn to write, button buttons, and brush his teeth with his left hand.

She understood that even with intensive therapy, significant disabilities would remain.

"I don't mean to sound cruel," she said slowly, "and this is embarrassing to admit, but I'm sometimes jealous of those wives whose husbands didn't come back. At least they can restart their lives."

Tears rolled down her cheeks. Then she added, "I sent this handsome young soldier to war, and I don't know this man who came back with his name."

She was being brutally honest, for trauma-caused disabilities are devastating, not just for the victims but for their families as well. Some families are not able to deal with the wounds, and they sometimes abandon the victim, leaving them alone and penniless.

I asked her, "What are you going to do?"

She wiped her eyes, sat up straight and strong, and replied with determination, "I made that decision on my wedding day. If it takes me 20 years, I will teach him to laugh and love again."

To laugh and love again ... isn't that what this is all about? We are all working through some sort of trauma, as we try to rebuild and have the best life possible.

YOU GET TO CHOOSE

Your renewal comes as you choose faith, trust, grace, and your mission. These are the final choices that lead to your health and freedom from your trauma.

You know that your renewal begins with faith. Applying faith as you walk forward is the challenge.

That starts with surrender, letting go of the old ways that don't work. They only feed your depression and anxiety anyway! The whole point of surrender is letting go so that you let God in.

Surrendering does not mean you are weak. I have had countless clients tell me that they feel they should be able to fix their own problems and find their own answers. They don't need any help, they don't want any help, all because help is considered a sign of "weakness."

> ## PAUL SPENT YEARS IN JAIL
>
> Today's jails are luxurious by comparison. Prisons then would have been dark, cold, filthy, infested with rats and insects; food would be minimal; and he likely would have been chained to a wall or in solitary confinement much of the time. He would have heard the anguished cries of fellow prisoners echoing off the stone walls.
>
> Imprisonment itself is associated with a higher likelihood of PTSD. For Paul, his time in jail seemed to only make him focus more on his mission.

HOW TO APPLY FAITH

Paul knew he could not escape the beatings and imprisonment by the Roman empire. So what did Paul do? He looked to God for help, so that he could maintain his faith and strength. He wrote:

> For God did not give us a spirit of cowardice, but rather a spirit of power and of love and of self-discipline (2 Timothy 1:7 NRSV).

That is how Paul applied faith. He wanted to *overcome* his torment, not *escape* it, and he did so by faith.

Paul's faith gave him the mental, physical, and emotional strength to endure anything thrown at him. He knew he was never alone, for God was always with him. (Likewise, you are never alone, for God is always with you.)

Throughout his life, Paul refused to be defined by his afflictions. His life was defined by his faith. He boldly stated:

> For our light and momentary troubles are achieving for us an eternal glory that far outweighs them all (2 Corinthians 4:17 NIV).

It is normal, with trauma, to be always looking for any signs of danger. Our radar is forever "on" to some extent, but with healing we no longer have to live in fear of attack.

However, we need to transform our view of life through our faith. This creates an entirely different way of looking at things. Instead of focusing on the day's troubles, we choose joy, we look for blessings, we see God at work in our lives, we know He is with us and sees our cures not our cuts.

That's how Paul chose to see his life, which is why he could write:

> Be joyful in hope, patient in affliction, faithful in prayer (Romans 12:12. NIV).

> Rejoice always, pray without ceasing, give thanks in all circumstances; for this is the will of God in Christ Jesus for you (1 Thessalonians 5:16–18 ESV).

> For we walk by faith, not by sight (2 Corinthians 5:7 NABRE).

Overcomers think this way, just as Paul described in these verses. To build your faith, practice Paul's short list:

- Be joyful.
- Be patient.
- Pray constantly.
- Rejoice always.
- Be grateful.
- Walk by faith.

Faith is the natural result. It gives new meaning to all experiences—past, present, and future.

Old ways of thinking (such as anger, isolation, and self-defeat) are quickly discarded. They have no place in you.

It was faith that gave Paul the ability to prevent any trauma from overwhelming him. Because he saw meaning in his sufferings, you could even argue that his horrific experiences, torture, and imprisonment never reached the level of "trauma" for him. And without trauma, there is no post-traumatic stress.

Didn't he call his troubles "light and momentary"? Only someone walking by faith could say such a thing.

While in jail awaiting his execution, Paul's faith gave him phenomenal clarity. Weighing the benefits of remaining alive or dying, he did not dwell on his losses. Rather, he saw advantages in both:

> I'm torn between two desires: I long to go and be with Christ, which would be far better for me. But for your sakes, it is better that I continue to live. Knowing this, I am convinced that I will remain alive so I can continue to help all of you grow and experience the joy of your faith (Philippians 1:23–25 NLT).

That's an overcomer, even in the face of death.

As you build your faith, I encourage you to build a support network around you. By that, I mean:

1. **Worship**: Find a church. Build your faith community inside and outside the walls of the church. Each house of worship has support for individuals, families, teens, women, and children. Find those and connect. Do not wait for it to find you.
2. **Build faith with friends**: Be real in your conversations. Ask each other questions. Seek answers. Grow together. Be there for each other in times of adversity, because that is where your words of faith turn into action.
3. **Read the Bible**: Your faith grows as you read God's Word. Because the problems of this world keep repeating themselves, the age-old answers are right there in print as if they were written for today. Have the courage to read it.
4. **Learn from others**: Those who have fallen and been renewed by their faith are excellent sources of help and wisdom. There are remarkable stories of recovery and renewal all around you.

5. **Grow your faith**: Work at your faith in those moments of silent solitude when you listen to God. Commit time each day to renew your faith. You are worth it.

As you apply faith, your faith will grow bigger than you ever imagined.

HOW TO APPLY TRUST

Right behind faith is trust. It is a necessary and wonderful part of your renewal. It also begins with a choice.

You may have heard about Jessica Buchanan, the school teacher who (back in 2011) was kidnapped in Somalia at gunpoint and held for ransom. Thankfully, she was rescued by Navy SEAL Team Six.

During her months in captivity, she finally understood what her had father meant when he was grieving the loss of his wife and said: "God, I don't understand you, but I am choosing to trust you."

She learned first-hand the fact that growth comes from trauma, and a big part of that growth comes from the decision to choose trust. Forged by the fires of trouble, her trust emerged as strength.

Paul understood that as well. He is the one who wrote these often-quoted words:

> I am not saying this because I am in need, for I have learned to be content whatever the circumstances. I know what it is to be in need, and I know what it is to have plenty. I have learned the secret of being content in any and every situation, whether well fed or hungry, whether living in plenty or in want. I can do all this through Him who gives me strength (Philippians 4: 11–13 NIV).

Both in good times and in bad, you can put your trust in the One who knows the way.

Paul's trust in God carried him through "tears and trials . . . through bonds and afflictions" (Acts 20:19, 23 ASV).

Paul did not get everything he wanted, or when he wanted it, but God's plans for him were fulfilled with what he needed, when he needed it. That's how trust in the Lord's plan works.

Is it hard for you to trust God? Is there something that stands in your way? Keep working at it. Fight through the doubts. You may not understand how the plans are working or even wonder why your prayers are not answered, but you can choose to trust that God has it figured out.

When it really comes down to it, trust really is a choice. Once you accept that decision, you need to do all you can to keep your trust strong.

These will help protect your trust:

1. **Commit**: Make up your mind that your attitude will be one of patience, strength, courage, and endurance. Let go of any distractions, especially anxiety or worry.
2. **Ask for help**: If the wounds of your past hurt your ability to trust, then find people or support groups where you can learn, listen, and ask real questions. Trust is not always easy, but there are many people who have run this race before you, so humbly asking for their help makes good sense.
3. **Be in the moment**: Focus on the now. The past is over and the future doesn't exist yet, so don't let anxiety or worries bring you down. Trust God in the now.
4. **Stay away**: Avoid places, people, and situations where you know your trust will be squashed or minimized. If it doesn't make your faith stronger, stay away.
5. **Grow in God**: Building a trusting relationship with God includes reading the Bible, praying, attending a healthy church, and finding people who will encourage you.
6. **Trust God with your problems**: Hand your anxiety and worries to God. Humbly, give it to God, and let Him handle it.

Paul trusted that God knew him, understood him, forgave him, loved him, and had a purpose for him. That trust is what gave Paul great strength! After all, his trust was not in himself, but in God!

HOW TO APPLY GRACE

Following faith and trust, your renewal requires grace. And as we have already discussed, grace is best described as a favor that is unmerited yet deserved, unending, unlimited, free yet priceless, and it completes us.

Grace is a lot of things, but people in the middle of trauma often feel anger, judgment, condemnation, vindictiveness, negativity, vengeance, or emptiness. When they need grace the most, they feel they are the least worthy of it.

Unfortunately, that stops most people . . . but it shouldn't!

You see, if you didn't need it, it wouldn't be grace. The very fact that you need grace should be the biggest green light to proceed forward toward grace. You have all the permission you need! It's there, waiting, in front of you.

As for the application of grace:

- The best time to apply grace is when you need it the most and the least.
- And the only way to apply grace is to open your arms wide and simply receive it.

I believe grace is a doorway that leads directly to unconditional, abundant, infinite love. Knock, and the door will be opened to you (Matthew 7:7 NABRE). Even when others may not accept you, you can still rebuild and renew your life knowing that the grace of God is offering you the opportunity for a new life. Of all of Paul's writings, perhaps the most quoted is his description of this gracious love:

Love is patient, love is kind. It does not envy, it does not boast, it is not proud. It does not dishonor others, it is not self-seeking, it is not easily angered, it keeps no record of wrongs. Love does not delight in evil but rejoices with the truth. It always protects, always trusts, always hopes, always perseveres. Love never fails (1 Corinthians 13:4-8 NIV).

It is grace that pulls you free from the power of trauma. You are freed to release toxicity, remove self-pity, crush fear, destroy arrogance, and reject despair. That worked for Paul, and the same will work for you.

Receive God's love. Grace sets you up to receive it. That's why Paul said:

And now these three remain: faith, hope, and love. But the greatest of these is love (1 Corinthians 13:13).

To keep the channel of grace open so that you can apply grace, these will help:

1. **Call for reinforcements**: Don't let yourself get distracted. Grace has the power to help you heal, but if you are depressed then you are understandably less confident. Do not let your hesitation prevent you from calling for help. God made you, but also created good people to help you along the way.

2. **Help others find grace**: Your presence has purpose. There are people around you who need grace as well. Tell them how you moved from victim to recovery to renewal. Offer inspiration and hope. Your presence alone is a reminder to them that they are not abandoned. You don't have to be perfect, just be there.

3. **Fill your words with grace**: Where others are discouraged, offer words of encouragement. If they feel unsafe, assure them of their safety. If you see them making a mistake, redirect

them. Instead of saying, "Don't be anxious," say, "I understand how you can feel that way; what helps you feel calmer?" Instead of diminishing their feelings with, "Sure it's bad, but someone always has it worse," say, "This must be difficult for you; what do you need?" Instead of dismissing them with, "Stop acting so weak," ask, "What makes you strong?" Instead of impatiently saying, "Hurry up and tell me what's wrong," say, "It's OK if you can't put it into words." Instead of rushing someone through grief by saying, "It's time you just moved on," demonstrate the patience of grace and say, "Take whatever time you need."

4. **Practice solitude**: It's difficult to feel grace when your life is filled with distracting background noise. Seek time to see, and listen where grace is in your life.

5. **Focus on the good**: Don't focus on your miseries. These are just more noises to block you from the awareness of grace. Ruminating on the gloom is not getting you any closer to healing. Pray for the qualities of grace for your recovery and renewal: patience, trust, hope, and perseverance.

6. **Practice gratitude**: No matter how desolate you feel, you still have some blessings. Be grateful. If you can't think of any right now, be grateful for what will be better in your future. If you are grieving, be patient with yourself. If you are helping someone through their grief, be patient with them. Gratitude is a resilient strength against suicidal thoughts.[1]

7. **Don't worry about the bumps**: On your journey of resilience, resistance, recovery, and renewal, you may still have times of weakness, fear, despair, and doubt. That's fine! Grace didn't go anywhere! God is right beside you. Keep going and ride over the bumps.

Applying grace is wonderful because it never ends. It's always there, full and ready for you.

HOW TO APPLY YOUR MISSION

After faith, trust, and grace comes your mission. It happens, and I believe it's part of God's plan for each of us.

One of my favorite examples of this is John Newton, who was born back in 1725. He is best known as the composer of the song "Amazing Grace," but that was only part of his mission.

Newton had his own trauma: the death of his mother when he was a young boy, pressed into service in the tough disciplined British Navy where he was flogged for desertion, humiliated to the point of considering suicide, despised by his shipmates for his arrogant behavior, treated as a slave in Africa, served on the crew of several slave ships, nearly drowned in a storm at sea, had his request refused to enter the Anglican priesthood, and more.

Personally, his life was an example of debauchery, drinking, and poor self-discipline.

Then, while on a ship in the middle of a storm, in fear of losing his life, he prayed for God's mercy. He vowed to turn his life around if God would give him another chance. He lived, and Newton began to make changes, though it took him several years to do so.

Eventually he gave up the slave trade and was even accepted into the clergy. While a priest, he wrote hundreds of songs, including "Amazing Grace."

But here is where his mission really grew. He became friends with William Wilberforce, a young member of the British parliament who wanted to leave politics and take up the ministry. Newton encouraged him to stay, convincing him that he could be of greater service if he stayed in parliament.

Wilberforce became an outspoken proponent of abolition, but he had difficulty gaining support and turning public opinion. To help the cause, Newton published a pamphlet in 1787 called

Thoughts Upon the Slave Trade. In it, he described his own witness to cruelty against slaves.

That pamphlet inspired public support for abolition, and Newton remained committed to the mission of abolition. In 1807, shortly before his death, the act to end the slave trade became law. Newton's mission spanned decades, and through it, he helped to end slavery, which arguably saved thousands and thousands of lives.

 Now You Know:

Failures aren't failures if you learn, adapt, and change. That's success!

He was the right man for the job, but he used his trauma as a stepping stone into his mission.

Obviously, we are not in Newton's time in history, but in our own way in our own world, we can make an impact. Riches, fame, and power are not required.

You can make an impact. You can do it with what you have and where you are. After all, you are equipped with strength, courage, hope, endurance, faith, and more. What you have experienced and learned the tough way can be an inspiration for others to break out of darkness and to never accept "impossible" as an answer.

Did you know that there are over 1.5 million charitable organizations registered in the United States alone, and that includes more than 40,000 military veteran service organizations? Millions of people volunteer their time and talents every year. While all of these people are healing others, some are healing themselves.

One person can make a difference. Your own mission can be as small as helping one person or as big as starting a major movement. It's up to you. There are no limits.

Paul well understood the impact that one person could make because he benefitted from that himself. His practical words give us many ways that we can make an impact:

Encourage the fainthearted, help the weak, be patient with them all (1 Thessalonians 5:14).

And we know that for those who love God all things work together for good, for those who are called according to his purpose (Romans 8:28 ESV).

Each person should live as a believer in whatever situation the Lord has assigned to them, just as God has called them (1 Corinthians 7:17 NIV).

For this purpose, He called you through our proclamation of the good news (Thessalonians 2:14 NRSV).

PAUL AND HIS MISSION

While on the road to Damascus, the Lord asked, "Why are you persecuting me?" and Paul immediately replied, "Lord, what do you want me to do?" The Lord said, "Arise and go into the city, and you will be told what you must do" (Acts 9:1-6 NKJV).

Paul said "yes" with his words and then took immediate action. The mission and the cost were made crystal clear from the onset, but Paul did not question, negotiate, or equivocate. He accepted his mission and remained committed to it for the rest of his life.

During his 30-year mission, every obstacle, setback, and disappointment only made him more tenacious, more determined, and more inspiring. I believe his mission-centered life played a big part in inoculating him from the negative effects of trauma.

What that looks like for you is part of the fun and freedom that you have! As you move forward with life and your mission, I suggest:

- Choose a mission that continues your growth.
- Start small. Every little bit of your time, effort, and money does count.
- Stay involved with your support community.
- If you volunteer with an organization, and the work opens old wounds, serve in another capacity or step away for a time. That is fine.
- With your experience, you can mentor others, perhaps even become a trained counselor.
- Just being supportive of others can be your mission, for true empathy is always encouraging and survival is always inspiring.
- Make sure your mission benefits you in some way. Thinking win-win is long-term thinking.
- Look for ways to help close to home. You can go overseas, but there are countless opportunities in your zip code where you can help.
- You have a lot to offer, so don't listen to any lies that would discourage you. Perfection is never required.

The whole point of your mission is you becoming who you are meant to be. As Roger Williams used to say, "The greatest crime in the world is not developing your potential. When you do what you do best, you are helping not only yourself but the world."

At the end of John's Gospel, he wrote: "There are many other things that Jesus did. If every one of them were written down, I suppose the whole world would not have room for the books that would be written" (John 21:25 ESV). John could have selected *any* closing story, but he chose one we can relate to. Imagine what it had been like for Peter, who three years earlier, was tired from an unsuccessful day of fishing when this stranger named Jesus stopped by and told them to cast their net on the other side of the boat. Their net was nearly bursting from the size of the catch. Jesus said, "Follow me."

They had no idea what they would be in for during the next few years, especially through those final days when Jesus was arrested, tortured, crucified, died, and rose again. What were they feeling now? Guilty? Stunned? Exhausted? Inspired? Confused?

In the wake of overwhelming events, we often return to a familiar activity just to reconnect with the comfortable. Peter did just that with something almost comical in its familiarity to us today. Peter said, "I'm going fishing." So, he and a few other disciples climbed into their boat.

But after being out all night their net was empty. Then, in the early dawn light, as the morning mist was lifting off the Sea of Galilee, Peter heard a voice from shore asking the question every bystander asks every fisherman: "Catch anything?" "No," they all replied. The voice told them to throw their nets on the other side of the boat. I imagine Peter thought what any frustrated fisherman would think: "Sure, why not?" So, he did. That's when their nets were filled nearly to bursting. Peter realized it was Jesus on the shore, jumped in the water, and swam the hundred yards to be with Him.

That swim to shore was a symbol of the baptism to wash off the old and be Renewed. And that question "Catch anything?" was so much more than just a fishing report. Jesus was asking Peter to do a personal checkup: "How's that fishing career working out for you?" Answer: it isn't and it won't. This was an important set up for Peter's new mission. Jesus then asked Peter three times, "Do you love me?" Each time, Peter answered "yes" and each time Jesus told him, "Feed my sheep." Saying it three times is a very big deal: a clear final instruction and a signed contract in triplicate. In other words, "Your fishing days are over. You have a new purpose. You are a fisher of men. Lead. Feed. Go. Do it."

So, too, if we are to commit to our renewal, we must let go of who we were. "Put on the new self, which is being renewed in knowledge after the image of its creator" (Colossians 3:10 ESV). Stop seeking comfort in the old ways. Stop fishing out of the wrong side of the boat. Stop seeking meaning in life by staying stuck in past miseries. Swim through the water and start fresh. We have a new purpose. We will make it. Press on.

Similarly, Paul's last message to Timothy advised him to press on in his own mission despite the pressure to give up, to endure the hardships, to commit to his mission (2 Timothy 4).

As for Paul, his ministry was complete, having persevered through years of trauma: "I have fought the good fight, have finished the race, I have kept the faith" (2 Timothy 4:7).

Learn from Paul and appreciate that the suffering done *to us* pales in comparison to the sacrifice accomplished *for us*. Paul dedicated his life to be worthy of *the* sacrifice: "No one has greater love than this, to lay down one's life for one's friends" (John 15:13 NABRE). Paul's commitment to that purpose made all the difference. He did not submit to depression. He celebrated with joy. And, this is all the more remarkable because his resilience, resistance, recovery, and renewal are absolutely true.

In our lowest point in life, you may no longer care about living, But the worst days of your life are the foundation for the best days ahead. Learn the powerful lessons from Paul, again and again and again and again. Build and rebuild your strength. Arm yourself with courage. Embrace hope. Accept the Faith, Trust, Grace and Mission given to you.

And be transformed by a renewing of your mind, knowing God's will for you is to be nothing less than the perfect version of yourself, healed and whole.

❋ ❋ ❋

From resilience to resistance and from recovery to renewal, you have come a long way!

PART THREE
Six Steps to STAY Healthy

Staying physically, emotionally, mentally, and spiritually healthy is everyone's goal! Sustaining trauma recovery requires a number of life changes.:

Step #5—Get Fit.
Step #6—Strengthen Your Attitude
Step #7—Get Enough Sleep
Step #8—Train Your Mind
Step #9—Eat Healthy
Step #10—Learn to Relax

PART THREE walks you through the steps to *stay* healthy. It's easy to remember, for each step fits into the F.A.S.T.E.R. model: Fitness-Attitude-Sleep-Train-Eat Healthy-Relax.

Chapter 12

Step #5—Get Fit

World-renowned neurosurgeon and team neurosurgeon for the Pittsburgh Steelers since 1982, Dr. Joseph Maroon collapsed into deep depression at the age of 41. He even left his medical career and began working at his family's truck stop. His recovery started when a friend coaxed him into a slow one-mile walk/jog around the local school track.

That evening, Maroon enjoyed his best sleep in many months.

Over time, he gradually increased the distance that he walked and jogged. Then he added other activities, such as swimming and biking.

The more he did this, the stronger he became and the less he was depressed. He started small, and it grew from there. Believe it or not, he went on to compete in a triathlon and then the infamous Iron Man Triathlon in Hawaii at 68! He returned to his medical career and advanced to international renown.

Fitness was the tool he used to get back on his feet, and he used fitness to help *stay* on his feet.

IT'S YOUR HEALTH WE ARE TALKING ABOUT

Your physical condition directly affects your brain condition. If your body is healthy, your brain is healthy. Conversely, if your body is out of shape and you feel like a slug, your brain can't help but be sluggish as well.

If you want to deal effectively with stress and trauma, the first step is to take care of your physical body. In fact, physical fitness is absolutely essential to staying healthy and free from the effects of trauma. Remember, stress and trauma harm your brain and body. Fitness is necessary for you to rebuild.

Over the years, I have worked with many people battling trauma who are trying to get physically healthy again. There is almost always a roadblock or two that must be dealt with.

If any of the following common roadblocks are a match for you and your situation, know that they are common and know that they can be overcome:

- Lack the motivation to get moving
- Not feeling worthy of better health
- See self-improvement as self-punishment
- Feeling lethargic from weight gain or medications
- Struggling with depression

 Now You Know:

You increase your resilience when you push yourself beyond your own expectations.

Recognize that virtually all limitations exist more in your head than they do in your body. The answer is to get up and move anyway.

I've seen amputees train for marathons and triathlons, which to me is proof that the greatest obstacles to getting physically fit are those of the mind. And if they can do it, you can do it.

START TODAY

You know it. We all know it. The best day to start working on our own fitness is always today.

Interestingly, our beliefs or thoughts about ourselves have the ability to actually turn up or turn down our physical abilities. It's truly a case of mind over matter.

I have seen many times where people performed far above their genetic or physical abilities simply because they believed they could. In fact, in studies where people were given false information on purpose, the subjects performed better or worse depending on that information. It wasn't real, but because they believed it, it became their reality.

In short, feelings and thoughts about your own limits really don't matter. Just get out there and start doing something to increase your physical fitness.

Working to improve your fitness levels is also beneficial because it is something you can control. Many things in life, especially the closer you are to your trauma, seem out of control. Being able to do some sort of exercise is a very concrete, physical step that you can take, and that is good for you in many ways.

When I was emotionally devastated and in the full grip of my trauma, I wanted nothing more than to remain in bed curled up in a fetal position. That was it.

Looking back, I wish I had known better. I would have told myself:

- Don't give up.
- Breathe deeply.
- Don't make any big decisions today.
- Get up.
- Move your body.

It is extremely difficult in the moment because the deluge of psychological pain is telling you that you are powerless to change, but that's not the truth.

🌱 *Now You Know:*

Fitness builds your physical/emotional strength, brain health, and self-discipline.

No, you don't have the power to change *everything*, but you do have the power to change *something*. The key is to act on the choices over which you do have control, even if those choices are little more than the choice to get out of bed, get dressed, and put one foot in front of the other with a walk down the street.

Stuck in bed, under the mental pressure to remain defeated, any exercise may seem to be of epic proportions. But you are in control.

This is urgent. Don't neglect it. Get up and move.

PAUL'S FITNESS

Some have speculated that Paul himself may have been a boxer or a runner because of his frequent references to sports. We don't know if he was, but we do know that he valued the routines of athletes to discipline the body in order to exert control of the mind.

He had first-hand knowledge of intense athletic competition because he spent time in Corinth (around AD 51–52), which was famous for its Isthmian games held every two years. Competitions included chariot racing, running, boxing, wrestling, and a brutal no-holds-barred combat sport.

For the athletes, physical training, self-discipline, and dedication were naturally the keys to winning. That is why Paul stressed the importance of constant striving for excellence:

> Every athlete exercises self-control in all things. They do
> it to receive a perishable wreath, but we an imperishable.

So I do not run aimlessly; I do not box as one beating the air. But I discipline my body and keep it under control, lest after preaching to others I myself should be disqualified (1 Corinthians 9:24-27 ESV).

Now You Know:

Prolonged stress and trauma are exhausting, but regular fitness activity reduces harmful levels of stress hormones.

Paul also emphasized the need to respect our own physical bodies as a means of glorifying God. If you receive a gift from someone who loves you, you take extra special care of it, which shows respect to the one who gave it to you.

For example, this could be as simple as hanging your child's first scribble on the refrigerator door as if it were a masterpiece in the Louvre. Or it may be the military medal a grandfather won during the war that he gives to his son or daughter when they enlist in the service.

The opposite also holds true, for when we discredit or reject the giver, we show incredible disrespect.

The gift that we have all been given is our body. And if we damage our body, it hurts the One who gave it to us. It shows ungratefulness and shortsightedness. And that only hurts us in the end.

Your body is a gift to you, and it is your responsibility to take care of it. Paul was the one who said it best:

Or do you not know that your body is a temple of the Holy Spirit who is in you, whom you have from God, and that you are not your own? For you have been bought with a price: therefore glorify God in your body (1 Corinthians 6:19-20 NASB).

For while bodily training is of some value, godliness is of value in every way, as it holds promise for the present life and also for the life to come (1 Timothy 4:8 ESV).

It is estimated that Paul walked over 10,000 miles during his many missionary travels. And during that time, he was frequently in danger of being robbed, beaten, and persecuted. He kept moving anyway. He wrote:

I have been in danger from rivers, in danger from bandits . . . in danger in the country (2 Cor. 11:26 NIV).

He never let any fears get in the way of him staying active.

FITNESS HELPS YOUR BRAIN

As you know, the brain controls so much of your body that it is vital it be in good health. Any and all physical fitness has a direct benefit to your brain.

- **New cells**: Our brain makes new cells daily. This neurogenesis is particularly active in the hippocampus (long-term and spatial memory) and the cerebellum (coordination and muscle memory).[1] Moderate to vigorous physical activity is one of the best ways to stimulate neurogenesis.
- **New growth**: Exercise activates a specific gene that promotes growth in the dendritic spine connections between cells.[2]
- **Brain function**: Aerobic fitness improves cognitive abilities, especially when done in conjunction with a healthy diet.[3]
- **Better scores**: Better cardiorespiratory capacity and muscle strength are associated with better academic scores among children and adolescents.[4]
- **Better memory**: One study[5] found that learning a list of vocabulary words was accomplished 20 percent faster by those

who were involved with intense physical exercise (running sprints) compared to those who were jogging or resting.

- **Improved learning**: The brain protein associated with this improved learning is brain-derived neurotrophic factor (BDNF), which prevents brain cell death, promotes brain cell connections, and supports cognitive function. My friend, former Pittsburgh Steeler and four-time Super Bowl Champion, Jon Kolb notes how exercise makes us more alert, attentive, and improves memory and thinking. He calls the effect of a good workout "Brain On Fire." It's true!
- **Bigger brain**: Unhealthy waist size is associated with a smaller brain size.[6] Higher levels of obesity are associated with loss of gray matter in the parts of the brain, affecting our control of movement[7] and the reward/motivation centers.[8] Burning fat builds the brain.
- **Less dementia risk**: A sedentary lifestyle contributes not only to obesity, but also to elevated blood pressure and higher cholesterol levels. These combine to increase the risk for dementia six-fold.[9]

Simply stated, your brain needs you to get up and go, and it rewards you for doing so.

FITNESS HELPS YOUR MOOD

Trauma and chronic stress often cause you to feel tired, lethargic, unmotivated, depressed, and even fearful. These can actually become debilitating, so your body needs you to take action now so you can shake off these symptoms.

The answer is to be physically active, for movement will change your mood.

- **Less anxiety**: Physical fitness is associated with a reduction of anxiety symptoms[10] and is a strong factor in the prevention of anxiety.[11]

- **Less depression**: A seven-year prospective study found those with lower aerobic and muscle strength are almost twice as likely to experience depression.[12]
- **Antidepressant**: BDNF and oxidative stress associated with exercise are believed to have an antidepressant effect.[13]
- **Less PTSD symptoms**: A review of 19 studies on PTSD reported an association between symptom improvement and exercise.[14] Fitness helps mood disorders so much that every treatment protocol for PTSD should include fitness.
- **Healthy children**: Children who actively participate in sports are significantly less likely to be withdrawn and depressed than their nonactive age mates.[15][16]
- **Decreased medication**: Anti-depressant medications are significantly less effective in persons who are obese.[17]
- **Builds Confidence:** Fighting stress requires energy and stamina and strength. Fitness is preparing you for bigger battles in life. "If you have raced with men on foot and they have worn you out, how can you compete with horses? If you stumble in a peaceful land, how will you do in the thickets of the Jordan" (Jeremiah 12:5).

FITNESS HELPS YOUR IMMUNE SYSTEM

The stronger your immune system, the healthier you are and the longer you are likely to stay that way. In short, the stronger the better!

Unfortunately, trauma brings stress, and stress damages your immune system. That's precisely why those with depression and anxiety get sick more often.

- **Restoration**: Even the most basic of physical exercise will help restore your immune system.
- **Better sleep**: Being active improves your sleep, and getting a good night's rest is imperative to restoring your immune system.

- **Less physical troubles**: By improving your immune system, physical ailments decrease and subside, directly reducing your number of physical troubles.
- **Higher white blood cell count**: A study on exercise and immunity found those who regularly rode bicycles had measurable changes in their immune system. Adult cyclists (ages 55 to 79) were compared with less active age mates and with less active 20 to 36-year-olds. White blood cells, which represent better immunity, usually decrease with age, but they were higher in the active older adults than their less-active peers and equivalent to the much younger but nonactive 20 to 36-year-olds.[18]

A SUPER SIMPLE THREE-STEP FITNESS PLAN

If something is too complex, we are less likely to do it. That is especially true when it comes to fitness. That is why this fitness plan is short, simple, easy to start, and easy to maintain.

Step #1—Just Start: Don't overthink it. You need it, and it's good for you in every way.

Step #2—Start small: Start with the possible. Choose an achievable goal that pushes you a little bit—not an overwhelming goal, like saying "I will work out for an hour every day for the next year." Step by step.

Step #3—Start where you are: Don't go on a spending spree to get new equipment or a new wardrobe. Join a fitness center if you want to, or don't. Whatever works, just take action.

HOW TO MAINTAIN YOUR MOMENTUM

As for what type of activity you will choose, it's up to you, but whatever you enjoy and will do is the best exercise program. Simple as that.

Now You Know:

Staying active is necessary for your physical, mental, emotional, and spiritual health.

Here are a few tips to help you keep up your momentum:

- **Do what's free**: Walking costs nothing, so take the stairs, walk farther to your car in the parking lot, or pick up the pace on your walk. Even mowing the lawn is good aerobic exercise.
- **Mix it up**: Include a little cardio, aerobic, and weights as you go. Maybe it's walking, biking, swimming, running, or using light free weights. Change things up to keep them fresh.
- **Keep adding**: Every step you take is progress against complacency. Add a few more minutes, reps, stairs, or laps to your routine, perhaps every week or every month. Over time, you will be amazed at your progress!
- **Push when you want to**: Some days you will want to push harder, longer, faster, more intense. When that happens, go for it. Greater intensity a couple of times a week is good, but not every day if being sore tempts you into quitting.
- **Schedule it**: Putting it on your calendar can help you stick to it. It's more of a priority.
- **Track your progress**: Write down what you did. This reinforces your success when you see all you've done.
- **Make it convenient**: Convenient, affordable, and fun are very important. If it's intimidating, too expensive, or too far to drive, you will inevitably quit. Your gym can be your home. There are plenty of options, including online training.
- **Do it with a friend**: If a friend will do this with you, it helps you both be accountable and motivated, and fights isolation.
- **Create healthy incentives**: Reward yourself (e.g., a workout shirt, more weights, new running shoes, new jeans, etc.) when you hit fitness milestones.

- **Find a coach**: If it helps you, hire a fitness coach who can design a fitness plan that is a perfect fit for your ability level. A coach can also be invaluable for encouragement and feedback. If you have any physical disabilities or medical issues, a certified trainer can give expert advice.

It takes about 90 days to really get into a routine and feel the results. Once you feel and see the results, you will be even more motivated to keep at it.

 Now You Know:

What should your heart rate (HR) be during cardio exercise? To calculate your maximum HR goal, subtract your age from 220. Your target HR is between 55 percent and 80 percent of that number.

I usually recommend a total of 2.5 hours per week of aerobic activity. Don't be frightened by that number, and don't start there. Instead, start small and grow. Work up to it, and if it takes you a while to get there, that's totally fine.

Remember, this is lifetime health and fitness we are talking about, not a rushed goal to be accomplished and then forgotten.

Keep the momentum going:

- **Good increases**: Exercise increases and improves your cardiovascular endurance, muscle mass, muscle power, strength, insulin sensitivity, memory, endorphins (improves your mood), and more.
- **"Bad" decreases**: Exercise decreases your weight, fatigue, depression, and recovery time.
- **Take a break**: If you need a break for a day or two, take it. Get back on your schedule as soon as possible. Stay focused on your goal and plan.
- **While traveling**: If you are on a road trip, try to stretch or walk a bit every hour or two. At airports, walk around

while waiting for your flight. Look for creative ways to keep moving.

- **Delete negative self-talk**: If you missed a day, didn't press as hard as you could have, or feel you didn't perform as well as you wanted, let it go. You are not a failure, not in the slightest. Don't listen to any negative self-talk. Simply put it behind you and move forward tomorrow.
- **You are in control**: If your exercise time keeps getting interrupted, pick a better time. You get to choose. This is your life.

PAUL HAD CUMULATIVE STRESS

Paul spent years traveling throughout present-day Israel, Turkey, Greece, and Syria on foot. Those years were not easy. He preached, converted, established churches, and dealt with questions and problems from those churches. It was a full-time intensive job that took him on journeys of several thousand miles.

Even after he left a town, his work was not complete. He often learned the churches he founded were being fractured by leaders who developed their own sects and rules. Paul had to settle questions and conflicts were passed on to him through oral and written communications, with limited information.

He had to wait weeks or months for a reply, which only added more stress. All the while he continued to travel, teach, and write while being hunted, lied about, tortured, robbed, hungry, and sleepless.

Compounding stress diminishes our ability to handle more stress effectively, while at the same time, it increases our vulnerability for physical and mental disease. Fitness fights cumulative stress.

WHEN TO TALK WITH A PHYSICIAN

There are times when you may need to talk with your physician. Don't hesitate. Your physician is there to help.

- **Medications**: If you take medications that have side effects that might affect your ability to do specific exercises, then choose an activity that is safer. For example, if a side effect is dizziness, then riding a stationary bicycle would be safer than a bicycle on the road. You still get the exercise, without any danger.
- **Pressure**: If you have symptoms that might be more affected by one type of exercise than another, then choose an activity that is less problematic. Or lower your weights, incline, or reps to your comfort level.
- **Tests**: There are many wearable options from watches to rings that objectively measure your heart rate and activity. Work with your doctor to track blood pressure, cholesterol levels, insulin, body mass index, testosterone, etc.

Chapter 13

Step #6—Strengthen Your Attitudes

I knew a boy who was constantly berated by his father, who called him "stupid" and mocked his idea of going to college.

The boy believed it, barely studied, consistently received poor grades, and even considered dropping out of high school.

One day at school, his class took a college aptitude test. When the results were mailed to his house, he opened the letter, saying he was actually in the top 1 percent!

Motivated by the test results, he began to study. His grades jumped up, and his confidence grew. His father even bragged to friends that his stupid son maybe wasn't so stupid after all.

Unfortunately, another letter arrived a few weeks later that said there had been a mistake, and that he had been mailed the wrong test results. Although his real scores were still above average, he was not in the top 1 percent as he had thought. His father promptly unleashed another barrage of insults on him about being a failure and now an embarrassment to the family.

At that point of devastation, with a natural slide back to poor grades and a pessimistic future about to happen, a supportive teacher wrote him a note that he would keep his entire life. He shared that letter with me, which read:

> The same young man got Ds one day and another day got As. The *only* difference is one day you did not believe in yourself, and another day you believed. Forget what everyone else says. Forget the insults, and dire predictions about your future. You were always told that you *could not*. Now you know it was only that you *would not*. Look what happened when you changed what you believe. Your attitude is your choice, no one else's. Never go backwards to failure. Keep believing in yourself.

What did the boy do? He chose to believe in himself.

Over time, his beliefs led to behavior change. The old emotions of despair were replaced by confidence. Hope grew. And he did go to college (which made his father proud), and he went on to be very successful in life.

The abrupt change to his life, and his future, came when he chose to change his way of thinking. His changed beliefs changed his emotions and his behavior. They are all connected.

WHAT ATTITUDE HAS TO DO WITH IT

At its core, attitude is a habit of thought. It's your habitual way of thinking. Scripture stated this truth thousands of years ago:

For as he thinks in his heart, so is he (Proverbs 23:7 NKJB).

Paul understood this principle as well, for he knew that not only is the battle first in the mind, but all change begins first in the mind.

Trauma can leave a mark on you, but continued trauma is not inevitable. Yes, the event influenced you, but it does not control you today, tomorrow, or next year. At this moment, I am not controlled by my past. And neither are you. Nobody is.

What that means is that you must decide how you want to live now. What will that look like? Where will you end up?

The answers depend on your attitudes today, for that determines the very thoughts you think . . . and from that flow your moods and actions . . . and from your actions flows the life you choose!

It's 1, 2, 3.

 Now You Know:

Attitudes are a connection of thoughts, feelings, and behaviors.

Here are a few unchanging facts to always remember:

- **Positive people**: Those with positive and optimistic mindsets are stronger, more resilient, and quicker to recover.
- **Negative people**: Those with negative mindsets are weaker, more vulnerable to selfishness, addiction, narcissism, and hurt, and improve much more slowly (if at all).
- **Outside forces**: We cannot change situations, people, or forces outside ourselves, but we can break the cycle of our own self-destructive thoughts and reactions.

The way to bring about the change you want is to first change your attitude. I have found, and I tell clients this all the time:

Whenever you are having a difficult time advancing forward in your battle, unhealthy attitudes are blocking your progress.

How is it that attitudes have such control over your life and your future? It's because everything is built upon your habits of thought.

DYSFUNCTIONAL WAYS OF THINKING

Because of trauma, in addition to our past choices and previous ways of thinking, we often need to recalibrate or adjust our thinking going forward.

In short, we may be going in the wrong direction. As soon as we are aware of that, we need to change course.

But here is a taste of reality . . . the need to tweak our way of thinking is a need that never ends. Like the onion and its many layers, so our thinking needs to be improved, layer by layer.

Is it not true that when you were 20 years old you were a little (or perhaps a lot!) embarrassed by your thinking at age 10? And at age 30, didn't your thinking at age 20 seem a little incomplete? And at age 40, suddenly you realized how off your thinking was at age 30? And at age 50, you can't imagine what you were thinking at age 40? And so it goes.

At every age, your thinking should still be maturing and im-proving continuously.

Paul recognized this life-long process. His words challenge us for a lifetime:

> Keep thinking on things above, not on things on earth (Colossians 3:2 NET).

Yes, trauma does have a special way of messing with your think-ing, but don't stay stuck with harmful thinking. Attitudes can get you into trouble when they are based on false information. When you believe the lies, you live these lies.

For example, if you find yourself thinking, "My problems are so much worse than that person's" or "I can never shake these beliefs I have about myself," those are signs of believing lies.

Or if you find yourself ruminating on trauma for long periods of time, that only makes depression and stress intolerance more persistent.[1] And that is also a sign that you need to change your way of thinking.

Or perhaps you've had a lifetime of abusive messages. If you are thinking that you have no options or no future or that you are destined to fail, that is clearly a lie! Change your thinking!

Don't ever become the lie. Challenge the falsehoods as you become aware of them. Hold fast to true thoughts, such as: "I am valuable" and "I am worthy." Meditate on scriptures that build you up. Let the truth set you free.

 Scripture Says:

Isaiah 40:31; Isaiah 54:17; Joshua 1:9; John 14:27; John 16:33; Romans 15:5; 2 Corinthians 4:16; Ephesians 4:29; Philippians 4:13

IRRATIONAL WAYS OF THINKING

Sometimes we can get caught in a mental whirlpool. In this stuck condition, we are more likely to believe things that are completely irrational. Breaking free is of course the goal, but to do so, we must first honestly evaluate our way of thinking.

Challenge your own thinking:

Over-generalizing: Do you take one fact and generalize it to other things where it doesn't belong? Maybe you failed or were disappointed, and you assumed that you would get the same results in the future. *This sounds like*: "I tried that once, it did not work out for me and it never will," or "That person criticized my work, they probably hate me."

All-or-none thinking: Do you see the world in black and white with no gray, so that it must be perfect or it's all wrong? Doing so causes you to miss the opportunity to come to terms with your own problems. *This sounds like*: "I'm not an alcoholic because an alcoholic is drunk all the time, I can stop drinking whenever I want, I've done it a hundred times" or "Since I had to remind my husband about what flowers I like, when he gave them to me, I was angry" or "Any good that happened in my past is erased by the bad."

Catastrophizing: When a problem comes up do you jump to the conclusion it's a total and permanent catastrophe? This makes problems far too big to overcome. *This sounds like*: "I will never recover" or "What has happened to me is the worst thing that has ever happened to anyone, ever!" or "I didn't get the job, I will never be successful."

Feel-Think: Do you assume your feelings are an accurate representation of what happened? This means if you feel something, it must be true, and that is dangerous. *This sounds like*: "My anger is proof that I am right" or "I know you don't love me because I don't feel your love" or "If I feel anxious then there must be something out there" or "I feel like I'm a burden on my family, so therefore I am."

Personalization: Do you distort the facts by putting the blame on yourself, even when others are to blame? This logic leaves no room for listening or advice. *This sounds like*: "My buddies were killed in that explosion because of me" or "It's all my fault I was abused" or "My mom got cancer because I'm not a good person" or "If I had been home this never would have happened."

Externalization: Do you blame everyone else and refuse to take any responsibility? This renders you powerless. *This sounds like*: "It's all their fault that I am upset because they are out to get me" or "I'm angry because he made me angry" or "There is nothing I can do to change the way I react to others" or "I drink because my parents were alcoholics" or "Any good that happens to me just happens; I have nothing to do with it."

 Now You Know:

The danger of believing lies is that you can eventually become those lies.

These irrational ways of thinking are at their peak in the middle of a mental whirlpool. Thoughts becomes so muddled that it's hard to break free.

A friend of mine suffered from PTSD. Avoiding crowds was his thing. Over the years, he skipped his children's parent-teacher meetings, sports games, and school plays. If there was an event, he didn't go.

He felt terrible about missing so much of his children's lives. You might think this would motivate him to change, but his shame actually had the opposite effect. What's more, he wouldn't listen to others, much less let his thinking change.

One day I asked him to write out his reasons for resisting change in this area. Here are the four reasons he wrote down:

1. If I can get better now, it's proof I could have changed earlier in life.
2. If #1 is true, it is proof I have failed my family earlier in life because I could have changed, but I did not.
3. If #1 and #2 are true, then I deserve punishment for not getting better.
4. Punishing myself includes not letting anyone get emotionally close to me.

Wow! In his mind, all of this made perfect sense, but you can see how his convoluted "reasoning" violated every rule of rational thinking.

Sadly, this is a very common line of thinking for those having trouble recovering from trauma.

I understand that when we are desperate, we will use whatever we can get our hands on to make it through the day, even if it does not work very well. Like in a boat with a leak, we think we can stay afloat if we just keep bailing out the water fast enough. But it is exhausting. Troubling thoughts and feelings will keep leaking in, requiring more and more energy. Then, as exhaustion grows, we risk erupting into a fit of anger, depression, panic, and suicide.

All of that from irrational thinking!

My friend needed to let go of his unhealthy thoughts. If you find yourself thinking like this, examine each thought as they come up, then discard them if they are not in line with where you want to go. Inch by inch, layer by layer, you can rebuild rational thinking into your life.

It's up to you. You get to choose.

HOW TO REPLACE HARMFUL THOUGHTS

The strongest motivation to change is always self-motivation. Anything and everything is possible when you want it badly enough.

So how exactly do you change the way you think?

The most common ways this happens includes learning as you go through life, from:

- Friends who point you in the right direction; and
- Professional counselors who walk you through the steps to change.

Some people will miss these obvious clues. They barrel forward until they experience something so devastating that they are forced to change. Sadly, they choose to change their thinking after a car accident, bankruptcy, loss of their home, their spouse leaves, a cancer diagnosis, friends walk away, getting fired, etc.

My dad did that. He finally got serious with his alcoholism and sought help when his health suddenly started to fail. Better late than not at all.

 Now You Know:

A healthy attitude is the foundation of mental strength.

But waiting for a shock-and-awe moment to make a change is not smart. What if it never happens? And usually, at that point it's too late. It's like realizing you missed the exit. Not only do you need to turn around, you have to make up the lost ground. But you cannot make up the lost time.

With that said, I believe the best and fastest way to move from unhealthy thinking to healthy thinking is through professional counseling.

Some may argue that their problems are too big to solve, but most are unwilling to share their private thoughts and would rather hold on to their defenses instead.

I've been counseled and I've been a counselor, and I understand the reluctance to talk, be honest, and ask for help. Why do we fight it?

Over the years, I've heard many excuses about not wanting to get counseling. Here are several of the most common:

1. If I ask for help, it means I'm weak or crazy.
2. I can't let others know I'm a failure.
3. I'm too ashamed to talk about what happened to me or what I did.
4. I'm not worthy of getting better, and I cannot be forgiven, so I should forever be punished for what happened.
5. I'm successful, so I must be OK.
6. It's the fault of others; they need help, not me.
7. This has been going on so long, I can't get better.
8. I'm strong; I can handle this on my own.
9. No one could possibly understand what I'm going through.
10. Talking about this will make me worse.
11. God is punishing me.

None of these excuses are true, but I hear them all the time. These attitudes are toxic barriers that block out healing.

In all honesty, I have said many of these to myself, and I realize now how these can become self-fulfilling prophecies for more decline.

But here is something to consider:

> The fact that we create false beliefs in our minds means we can uncreate them.

Nobody is born with these beliefs, or any faulty belief for that matter. We learn them.

It's time to fight back and choose the attitudes and thought patterns that you want to live your life with. Replace the previous false excuses with these true statements:

1. Asking for help is a sign I am strong.
2. Strong emotional reactions to trauma are normal.
3. I refuse to let this ruin my life anymore; I am taking control.
4. I am worthy. I am not broken. I am not a mistake. I do not have to keep punishing myself. I can be forgiven.
5. I am capable of being emotionally successful. I hurt, and I want to get better. Denial won't change my life.
6. Even if others share the blame, I am focusing on my own recovery.
7. No matter how long this has troubled me, I am going to get better.
8. Successful people ask for help, too. We can all improve.
9. There are others who do understand, who care, and who can guide me through this, even if they do not know my exact troubles. I am not alone.
10. Misery is my choice and is not permanent. I am taking charge.
11. God is not abandoning me. God wants me back. I am loved by God unconditionally, eternally.

Those true statements are so much better! They bring peace, encouragement, and hope.

HOW DID PAUL THINK?

Paul had his own shock-and-awe experience on the road to Damascus that brought profound changes in his life. But he was able to endure decades of taunting, threats, pain, beatings, torture, trials, and impending death.

PAUL SUFFERED CHRONIC PAIN

Paul suffered from something that kept him humble. We don't know exactly what this "thorn" in his flesh was, but we do know that it plagued him his entire life.

He wrote: "Because of the surpassing greatness of the revelations, for this reason, to keep me from exalting myself, there was given me a thorn in the flesh, a messenger of Satan to torment me—to keep me from exalting myself!" (2 Corinthians 12:7 NASB).

Chronic physical or emotional pain wears us down, making us more susceptible to illness and depression, and making us more vulnerable to the temptation of bad choices. The National Institute for Healthcare Excellence estimates that about 31 percent of the US population has chronic pain, and half of those cases also have a diagnosis of depression.

Clearly, Paul was very purposeful and careful with the habits he chose for his thoughts. Here is a little insight into that:

We do not want you to be uninformed, brothers and sisters, about the troubles we experienced in the province of Asia. We were under great pressure, far beyond our ability to endure, so that we despaired of life itself. Indeed, we felt we had received the sentence of death. But this happened that we might not rely on ourselves but on

God, who raises the dead. He has delivered us from such
a deadly peril, and he will deliver us again (1 Corinthians
1:8–10 NIV).

Paul could withstand all of this because he knew how to
create the habits of thought (his attitude) that would sustain
him.

Interestingly, a nineteenth-century philosopher and psychologist by the name of William James famously stated, "The greatest
discovery of my generation is that a human being can alter his life
by altering his attitudes."

Paul knew that truth almost 2,000 years earlier. What's
more, Paul lived by it, and that is what kept him healthy and
strong.

Epictetus, a Stoic philosopher and contemporary of Paul,
taught that it is not things or events that upset us, rather, it is
how we think about them that determines our response.

Arrian, a student of Epictetus, described how our view of our
infirmities is our choice:

Sickness is a hindrance to the body, but not to your ability to choose, unless that is your choice. Lameness is a
hindrance to the leg, but not to your ability to choose.
Say this to yourself with regard to everything that happens, then you will see such obstacles as hindrances to
something else, but not to yourself.[2]

Paul's own words really illustrate the foundation of modern
psychological counseling. Anyone who thinks it's something recently discovered hasn't read Paul:

And do not be conformed to this world, but *be transformed
by the renewing of your mind,* so that you may prove what
the will of God is, that which is good and acceptable and
perfect (Romans 12:2).

This truth Paul has stated can be applied to your life this very moment. Look at it this way:

1. You do not have to go along with what the world is telling you.
2. You can transform the way you think by "renewing" your mind daily (constantly).
3. Your irrational thoughts can be (and must be) replaced with proper beliefs.

PRACTICE HEALTHY THOUGHTS

Habits form over time, and they are a direct result of the choices you make. Because attitude is a habit of thought, it is vital that you choose the habits you want.

When my little granddaughter was first diagnosed with a rare, aggressive, and late-stage cancer, it was devastating news for all of us. My daughter said "The four words no parent ever wants to hear are 'your child has cancer'." Our dreams of a joy-filled future with this delightful little four-year-old came to a screeching halt.

Daily family routines switched from driving her to preschool to driving to doctor visits, taking medicines, hospital stays for chemotherapy, and fighting infections. The annoyance of brushing her tangled hair when she was three, seemed so ridiculous to get upset about when she lost all her hair at age four. We were angry and frustrated as long as we resented the loss of what was, and remained consumed with worries about what might be ahead. We could not change her cancer, but we could change our beliefs and actions. We all embraced attitudes of faith, hope, and trust to heal our hearts as she underwent her own physically healing treatments.

Paul understood this act of choosing the thoughts we make into habits, for he wrote:

> We are destroying speculations and every lofty thing raised up against the knowledge of God, and we are

taking every thought captive to the obedience of Christ (2 Corinthians 10:5 NASB).

Here are four choices that will lead to the healthy thoughts you want:

Habit Choice #1—Replace as needed. Throw out the garbage! Replace any and every thought, pattern, way of thinking, or mindset that you know is not healthy. Get a broom and sweep out the dark corners of your mind where old painful memories or self-defeating beliefs have settled.

Habit Choice #2—Change your heart. Quit demanding that the universe change to fit your wishes. Accept there may be purposes unknown to you. Seek a change of your heart, as Proverbs 23:26 says, "Give me your heart, and let your eyes observe my ways."

Habit Choice #3—Choose hope and prayer. You can always choose hope. That can never be taken away from you, no matter the circumstances. That is the foundation of healthy thoughts, so always choose hope, and never let it go.

Habit Choice #4—Be optimistic. Optimism is a choice. Living with pessimism only leads to prolonged pain, hurt, weakness, and dead ends. Choose the opposite! You want to live strong, grateful, healthy, and full of faith? Then make optimistic thinking your daily habit. Do not be captive to bitterness and sin (Acts 8:23).

 *Scripture Says:*

Proverbs 1:1-33; Proverbs 15:13; Matthew 5:1-11; Matthew 6:25-35; Luke 6:20-23

Chapter 14

Step #7—Get Enough Sleep

To avoid his nightmares, Ben would push himself to stay awake until he collapsed from exhaustion, or he would drink large amounts of alcohol until he fell asleep. The goal to avoid those nightmares affected everything in his world.

When we met, this had been going on for over ten years. I was amazed that his body had been able to withstand the treatment he was putting it through.

Our bodies cannot get restorative sleep when we are drunk, but somehow Ben managed to stay alive, employed, and married—but barely. He wanted to be free of the nightmares and to sleep peacefully, but he was stuck in a loop that he couldn't get out of.

To change his night, he needed to change his day. And to change his day, he needed to change his night.

We did just that. Today, saying that Ben is a new man would be an understatement.

SLEEP IS IMPORTANT!

Shame, regrets, and self-loathing all grow in nightmare-filled sleepless nights. That's partly why I was amazed that Ben had been able to keep his life more or less together for so long. His grit and determination, and incredibly patient wife, were no doubt the glue that kept things together.

Sleep disorders are characteristic of PTSD, and the lack of sleep increases the risk of other physical, mental, behavioral, and emotional problems.

Simply put:

> To heal and to stay healthy, your body needs a good night's sleep.

Typically, we push ourselves and cut corners on our sleep. It was Thomas Jefferson who said, "The sun has not caught me in bed in 50 years."

But no matter how hard we push ourselves, adults require about seven to nine hours of sleep per night. Some may be biologically programmed to function pretty well on less sleep, but most of us still need those seven to nine hours to maintain good health.

Adolescents during their growth spurts need even more sleep than adults, but teens seldom get enough sleep, as they stay up late studying or socializing with friends. As you would expect, excessive use of social media is linked with poor sleep and increased anxiety/depression,[1] but this fact applies to adults as well.

 Now You Know:

The military recognizes sleep can be weaponized against an enemy. So don't weaponize your own sleep deprivation against yourself.

Sleep problems include insomnia (getting too little sleep), too much sleep (hypersomnia), trouble falling asleep, and trouble waking up. They should be evaluated by a physician to rule out any medical causes such as sleep apnea.

About 30 percent of the US population reports occasional symptoms of insomnia, and 15 percent reports chronic insomnia.

Insomnia is not simply having a couple bad nights of sleep. Rather, insomnia is:

1. Regularly having difficulty falling asleep;
2. Waking up several times throughout the night;
3. Waking up early and not being able to get back to sleep;
4. Experiencing this for weeks on end.

Not getting enough sleep is simply bad for your health. Here are some scary statistics that will make you want to get your seven to nine hours of sleep:

- Sleep problems have been linked to anxiety and depression.[2]
- Adults who regularly get less than six hours of sleep per night are at greater risk for developing dementia with age, while seven hours or more is associated with a lower risk.[3]
- Chronic insufficient sleep is also associated with an increased appetite, decreased energy, and risk for diabetes.[4]
- Getting less than six hours of sleep per night is associated with a two-fold increase in cognitive impairment, hypertension, heart disease, and stroke.[5]
- One in 25 drivers report they have fallen asleep while driving in the previous month,[6] and 10 percent of accidents are associated with drowsy driving.[7]

If your work requires you to be up late or even awake all night, such as shift work, on call, or rotations, then do what you can when you can to catch up on sleep the next day.

Don't be the sleepless hero and push yourself beyond what your body can take. Your body will pay for it eventually.

SLEEP IS GOOD FOR YOUR BRAIN AND BODY

The brain is always busy, but believe it or not, it needs downtime to literally clean up (like your dishes after dinner). Waste is created by brain cells burning energy during the day. During sleep, changes in support cells allow the garbage to be flushed out of the system through the veins.

Restorative sleep benefits your body in many ways:

1. **Reduced depression**: Sleep increases serotonin levels, and that decreases depression.
2. **Mental clarity**: Sleep improves your attention, alertness, and problem-solving skills.
3. **Better memory**: Sleep helps your brain consolidate memories and learning, which gives you better memory.
4. **More happiness**: Sleep decreases anger, sadness, anxiety, and apathy.
5. **Stronger immune system**: Sleep strengthens the immune system, reduces inflammation, and improves blood pressure, and cardiovascular health.
6. **Weight loss**: Sleep helps balance your hormones, which helps with weight loss.
7. **Human Growth Hormone release**: Human growth hormone (HGH) is produced in the pituitary gland and is released when you are in deep sleep. It helps your cells grow and repairs damaged tissue. HGH levels in the blood are reduced when you are sleep deprived. Risk for obesity, heart disease, and diabetes increase with low HGH levels.
8. **Longer life**: Less than six or more than nine hours of sleep per night actually shortens your life span.

TRAUMA AND SLEEP

As you well know, trauma has a negative effect on your sleep, and the lack of restorative sleep only worsens the impact of stress and trauma.

It is said that trauma leads to sleep-disrupting bedtime anxiety. That means reliving traumatic memories, worrying we may not get better, and rehearsing anxious attitudes, all of which delay sleep, increase night wakening and reduce the number of hours of sleep.[8]

Did you know that only 10 percent to 30 percent of people exposed to trauma who *do not* develop PTSD will have a sleep disorder? But 94 percent of those who develop PTSD will have a sleep disorder!

Getting sleep in the first 24 hours after a traumatic event can actually help our brain process distressing memories better,[9] including the reduction of PTSD symptoms.[10]

Long after the initial trauma, getting sufficient sleep each day is essential for your health. Without it, the damage from poor sleep adds up.

Paul had more than his share of sleep struggles:

> I have been in labor and hardship, through many sleepless nights, in hunger and thirst, often without food, in cold and exposure (2 Corinthians 11:27).

Through his studies, Paul was very familiar with themes of sleep and rest throughout the Bible, including:

> In peace I will both lie down and sleep; for you alone, O Lord, make me dwell in safety. Restful sleep comes when we can set aside the worries of the day and place our trust instead that we will be safe (Psalm 4:8 ESV).

> Sweet is the sleep of laborers, whether they eat little or much; but the surfeit of the rich will not let them sleep (Ecclesiastes 5:12 NRSV).

The value of rest on the Sabbath was amplified in Paul's writing:

> There remains, then, a Sabbath-rest for the people of God; for anyone who enters God's rest also rests from their works, just as God did from his (Hebrews 4:9–10 NIV).

Paul carried a heavy workload between his ministry, travel, tentmaking, and writing. In our society, we praise those who are constantly "burning the candle at both ends." Working hard is valuable, but we will be of little value to others if our sleeplessness hits toxic levels.

Work hard, yes, but prioritize your time to let your brain and body recover through restorative sleep.

Paul's formula to get rest in the midst of trouble included praying. He said we should "pray without ceasing" (1 Thessalonians 5:17 NRSV). In the middle of the night, praying calms your spirit, pushes fears and thoughts aside, and helps you be at peace.

And that is a good recipe for falling asleep!

 Now You Know:

Most sleep problems are caused by:
- *Anxiety, worry, fear;*
- *Panic attacks, depression, hallucinations, delusions;*
- *Poor sleep routine;*
- *Medication side effects;*
- *A genetic condition;*
- *Heartburn, diabetes, kidney disease, thyroid disease, chronic pain, sleep apnea, or other physical health disorders.*

DOS AND DON'TS FOR BETTER SLEEP

Here is a practical list of things you should and should not do if you are trying to get a better night's sleep:

1. **DO schedule it**: Arrange your schedule so you can get at least seven to eight hours of sleep each night.
2. **DON'T eat a big meal before bed**: Food needs about three hours to go through digestion. A sugary or high-carb snack before bed will wake you up (and cause weight gain). Train

yourself to stop eating at least three hours before going to bed.

3. **DO set the mood**: Keep it dark, quiet (use a fan or white noise machine if needed), and keep your bedroom temperature on the cool side (68° to 73° F).

4. **DON'T leave the TV on**: People like to fall asleep to the sound of the TV, but it can wake you up during the night.

5. **DO give your eyes a break**: The light from cell phones and computer screen fools your brain into thinking it's daytime, so quit using them a couple of hours before going to bed.

6. **DON'T drink caffeine before bed**: The half-life of caffeine is about six hours, so give caffeine plenty of time to get out of your system. If you use a caffeinated preworkout drink, move your workout to as early in the day as possible.

7. **DO establish a routine**: Train your body to welcome sleep. It's not the time for distressing phone calls to an old flame or a dysfunctional family member. Do some mundane cleaning chores around your house or apartment. Relax with a hot bath/shower. Read a calming book before bed. If you start to nod off, stop reading, place a bookmark in the book, and go to sleep. As part of your bedtime routine, start to dim the lights in the house an hour or so before bedtime.

8. **DON'T text or email in the middle of the night**: Trying to think clearly (you don't want to be embarrassed in the morning) will only wake you up.

9. **DO think positive thoughts**: It's normal to wake up at night. If you do, review your gratitude list, stay in bed, think positive thoughts, pray.

10. **DON'T stay on sleeping pills**: Sleep aids such as zolpidem (Ambien) are meant for you to take a couple of times or to help readjust your sleep schedule after a flight that takes you through multiple time zones. They are not meant to be taken for long periods. Prolonged use can actually cause insomnia.

11. **DO exercise daily**: Exercising 20 to 30 minutes a day helps you sleep at night.

12. **DON'T surf the internet**: Late-night scrolling through social media apps, gaming, gambling, pornography, and impulsive buying will disrupt your sleep. Don't do these, period.

13. **DO meditate before bed**: If you are burdened by stress or nightmares, calm your body and brain with meditation, breathing exercises, or systematic relaxation.

14. **DON'T drink heavy alcohol before bed**: Some wine with dinner is one thing; however, while heavy drinking as self-medication to knock you out may get you to sleep, it blocks deep sleep, reduces restorative sleep, messes with memory formation, aggravates breathing problems (like sleep apnea), and makes you get up more often in the night to use the bathroom.

15. **DO progressive relaxation**: Once you get into bed, go through this routine:
    a. Box breathe (inhale slowly for four seconds, hold for four seconds, exhale slowly for four seconds, hold for four seconds; repeat four times or more).
    b. Relax your face muscles (include eyes and mouth).
    c. Progress to relaxing your shoulders and then your arms, one side at a time.
    d. Relax legs and feet.
    e. Relax your mind with your own personal calming images (such as a lake or warm cozy place like a hammock).
    f. Clear your head of negative thoughts, and repeat your own calming personal mantra or a very brief soothing book passage or poem.

16. **DON'T take long naps**: If you need to nap during the day, take a brief one (10–15 minutes, no more than 45 minutes) in the late morning or early afternoon. If you are exhausted after work, go to bed early.

17. **DO read the Bible**: Going to bed with scripture in mind is good for your heart, mind, body, soul, and sleep. Make it a habit to end the day in the Word.

18. **DON'T work late at night**: Mental work wakes you up and turns on your brain, so if you are working late, try to quit at least two hours before going to bed. You need time to calm back down.

19. **DO take natural sleep aids if needed**: Herbal teas, melatonin, and cherry juice can be helpful, but try not to use them every night. Natural sleep aids are not regulated, so review the contents and possible side effects carefully. As always, check with your doctor if you have any questions.

20. **DON'T stress**: If you wake up at night, pray or quote scripture. Turn sleepless time into prayer time or meditation. If you still can't sleep, get out of bed and read a paper book in a dimly lit room. Focus on quiet and calm activities.

21. **DO keep paper and pen by your bed**: If you have an idea at night, jot it down. Don't turn on your phone as the bright lights will blast you awake.

22. **Do silence your phone**: Turn off the volume so text messages or calls will not wake you up. If you can, keep your phone in another room at night.

Fixing sleep problems really comes down to *avoiding* what hurts your sleep and doing what *helps* your sleep. Pretty simple on the outside, but you would be surprised how many people struggle with a good night's sleep.

Remember, missing one or two nights of sleep is not a sleep disorder. Sleep problems are those that last several weeks or months, and require corrective action as quickly as possible so that your body can get the sleep it needs.

Make it your goal to get enough sleep. Work at it. Your good health demands it.

 *Scripture Says:*

Psalm 4:4; Psalm 65: 5-13; Psalm 121; Psalm 139:7-18; Proverbs 6:10; Ecclesiastes 5:12; John 14: 1-3

Chapter 15

Step #8—Train Your Mind

A ndrea was a respected ICU nurse. At age 28, aspiring to become a hospital administrator, she started taking night
classes toward a master's degree.

Walking to her car after class one night, she was assaulted
and robbed. Although she quickly recovered from her physical injuries, nightmares stole her sleep and her grades
plummeted.

Rather than fail her graduate program, she took a leave of absence from school.

At work, she began to have trouble concentrating and became
increasingly worried that she would make a mistake with a patient. To compensate, she obsessed over the details, often double
and triple checking her work.

Her lack of sleep and obsessive actions increased her exhaustion levels. Anxiety multiplied, and she began to experience
panic attacks. Worried she could no longer safely do her job,
she quit.

Sadly, her story is not uncommon, for her symptoms are typical of someone who has experienced trauma.

SOMETHING IS MISSING

You already know that trauma victims are more likely to suffer problems with health, sleep, weight, social relationships, and mood disorders. You can add learning difficulties, memory challenges, and concentration problems to that list as well. The following will probably not surprise you at all:

- Veterans with PTSD have higher unemployment and underemployment rates, more absenteeism, difficulties with workplace demands. Unemployed veterans with PTSD have more severe symptoms than those who are employed.[1,2]
- Grade school students who experience trauma also perform lower on standardized tests. One study found that students with a history of trauma were receiving special education services at a rate nearly three times that of the nontraumatized students.[3]
- The largest mass tragedy in Norway since World War II occurred in 2011, when a gunman dressed as a policeman entered a youth camp on an island and killed 60 people in about an hour. High school students who experienced the trauma declined in their school grades, had a higher absentee rate, and 26 percent dropped out of high school. Grades improved, however, for those students who remained in school and took part in school-based interventions.[4]

Trauma has a way of attacking our ability to focus and remain focused. As chronic stress negatively impacts the brain, our ability to form new memories is impaired, and our verbal processing skills are weakened. This hurts our ability to complete tasks, especially ones that require planning and reasoning.

I've explained this to my clients many times over the years. They usually look at me and say,

No wonder I get confused, overwhelmed, distracted, and walk around in a mental fog all day!

Over time, daily routines become more difficult. Forgetting names, losing things, and getting lost on the way to familiar places become increasingly common. With this mental decline, many are scared that they have early signs of dementia at age 30 or 40!

But it's not dementia. And it's not time to give up.

It is, however, time to strengthen an area of your life that will give you answers, help, options, health, and freedom.

 Now You Know:

Those who are victorious over stress and trauma are also dedicated to their own mental training.

THE NEED FOR TRAINING

The training we are talking about is the training of your brain. It's purposeful, beneficial, and even enjoyable. Here are a few of the many ways that this type of training helps you:

- Restoring your brain and body;
- Increasing your stamina for stress;
- Sharpening your attention;
- Increasing your concentration;
- Improving your memory;
- Better problem-solving skills;
- Improving your resilience, resistance, and recovery.

Ever wonder why the big barrel on a concrete mixer truck is always turning? The continuous movement prevents the mixed cement from hardening. But as soon as it stops, that cement will begin to harden.

The exact same thing happens with your brain. Move it or lose it!

With your brain, as it relates to training, we know two very important facts:

#1—Stress changes your brain for the worse. Chronic stress wears down your brain with real or imagined threats. This constant stimulation keeps your brain on high alert. Over time, this will strain, weaken, and burn out parts of your brain.

#2—Training changes your brain for the better. When you use your brain, blood flow increases in the areas being used and that generates new cell growth. New connections are made between memory cells as you use them. Simply put, when the brain fires, it wires, and that is great news for you.

All of this is evident when you see people who are overwhelmed with shame and fear, who then also struggle with concentration, memory, and problem-solving. One leads to the other.

If people don't take action at this point, things often get worse. I've seen people lose hope that things will never improve, and then they drift down into isolation, silence, and avoidance, which only compounds the problems they had to begin with.

Thankfully, this doesn't have to be the case. With the right training, you can recharge, rebuild, and restore. You can get healthy and stay healthy.

WHAT COUNTS AS "TRAINING"?

The more you train, the more it helps you. That makes good sense. But what exactly is this "training"?

You will be glad to hear that training counts as anything you want from these three categories:

#1—Get better: Practice getting better at what you already know.

#2—Add more: Choose different subjects or parts that branch off what you already know.

#3—Do new: Learn something entirely new that is not related to anything you currently know.

Now You Know:

Sufficient sleep, less stress, and good nutrition will increase your brain volume and cell connectivity.

Competitive athletes don't just show up on the day of competition. They are constantly training —and that means getting better, adding more, and doing new things. It's a continuous process of staying in shape in every way possible, so that they are ready on game day.

You don't have to be an athlete to apply this same winning formula to your own life. So, what will it be?

- Play an instrument? Learn new songs.
- Haven't played baseball in years? Hit the batting cages.
- Never had time to learn to paint? Take a class.
- Ride a horse.
- Learn to fly.
- Write a book, poetry, journal.
- Learn a new language.
- Read those books you've always wanted to read.
- Take college courses.
- Try a new sport.
- Rebuild a car.
- Attend lectures or watch online.
- Get certified in something that interests you.
- Travel.
- Play problem-solving games.
- Start a new hobby.

You can do anything that challenges and sharpens your mind with healthy learning. It all counts!

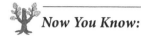
Now You Know:

Working on something meaningful reduces stress, keeps us on a schedule, builds self-discipline, and improves sleep.

PAUL VALUED TRAINING

Paul valued training, and was fortunate enough to study under the renowned Rabbi Gamaliel. Paul's yearning to master scripture became the foundation he would need throughout his life, especially in teaching, in his debates, and in his trials.

His proficiency was reflected in his later writings:

> For everything that was written in the past was written to teach us, so that through the endurance taught in the Scriptures and the encouragement they provide we might have hope (Romans 15:4).

After Paul's experience on the road to Damascus, there is an information gap of 10 years, where we don't know what Paul was doing. Knowing how much he valued scripture, and knowing he believed Jesus was the promised Messiah, we believe he spent those years further researching, discussing, and refining his understanding that Jesus was the fulfillment of the prophecies.

These years immersed in training his mind would be the same action he prescribed for others, particularly his mentee, Timothy. This training was vital. Paul advised Timothy:

> Carefully study to present thyself approved unto God, a workman that need not be ashamed, rightly handling the word of truth (2 Timothy 2:15 D-R).

The wording here is important. Other Bible translations of "careful study" refer to being "diligent" (NASB) or to "do your best" (NIV, NRSV) or to "work hard" (NLT).

Paul encouraged Timothy to not only learn but also aim to do his best. That way he would not need to worry about being ashamed in any way.

On your training journey, others will question you, some out of curiosity and some out of envy. Just don't let anyone be a barrier to your success.

I once heard a mom tell her teen son that she had decided to chase a dream and go to college. The son said, "You'll be 49 years old when you graduate."

She replied, "I'm going to be 49 anyway. Why not have something to show for it?"

Well said!

Whatever it is you want to do, dive in. It doesn't matter where you start. What matters is that you chase your dreams.

Retired Marine Sergeant Kirstie Ennis is a good example. She was wounded in a helicopter crash in Afghanistan, which resulted in severe injuries to her spine, leg, arms, shoulder, face, jaw, and brain. She would eventually have a leg amputated above the knee.

By her own admission she was caught in the quicksand of her mental and emotional wounds. She attempted suicide on the anniversary of her crash. During her lowest point, her father asked her, "The enemy couldn't kill you, and you are going to do it for them?" His question woke her up and got her back on the path to recovery.[5]

From that moment on, she focused on training hard to become a world-class Paralympian on the snowboard. She even climbed Mount Kilimanjaro. Today, she runs a foundation to support other veterans in healing through athletic challenges.

Don't let anyone keep you from your dreams!

And if you have trauma or stress to contend with, it is all the more important that you jump into whatever training you want. For you, it's vital.

PAUL USED HIS TIME WISELY

Paul's imprisonment in Rome during the last two years of his life (AD 60 to 62) was a house arrest. There he could write and receive visitors. Luke often met with him, and their conversations provided much of their history documented in the book of Acts. During this time Paul wrote a number of letters now included in the New Testament (Ephesians, Philippians, Colossians, and Philemon).

Being able to work, to minister from a distance, and to have visitors certainly gave him some comfort. But his impending execution still loomed over him. He did not complain of bitterness or fear. Instead, he wrote he would be happy whether he lived (so he could continue his ministry) or died (when he could be with Christ for eternity).

His words were, "But if I am to live on in the flesh, this will mean fruitful labor for me; and I do not know which to choose. But I am hard-pressed from both directions, having the desire to depart and be with Christ, for that is very much better" (Philippians 1:21-23 NASB).

TRAINING HELPS TRAUMA RECOVERY

Why is training necessary? Why is it so hard to learn new ways to handle old trauma?

Our brains are quick to develop patterns or grooves to handle trauma and chronic stress. These habits are supposed to be for our own good, except sometimes that is not the case. Bad habits are never going to bring good results.

Here are a few of these habitual thought patterns from people who are battling trauma:

- "Because of what I did, I am not worthy of success."
- "If I do something other than mourn 24/7, I am dishonoring the sacrifices of the others."
- "While others suffer (e.g., a child with cancer), I must suffer too."
- "I don't fit in, how could anyone like me?"
- "My life is hopeless, I should end it."
- "How could anyone forgive me?"

These negative thought patterns are habits that must be broken. If not, they will continue to get the same bad results for those who keep the habits in play.

Break the habits, and you do that with training.

I have seen hundreds of people experience successful growth after trauma. The simple act of choosing training to get better, add more, or do something new helped them break free.

And it's not all about leaving their past behind them. They strengthened themselves and rose to new levels, often far beyond what they ever thought possible. Their past may have been reduced to rubble, but instead of being buried under the debris, the broken stones became a foundation for a new life.

Upon the trauma, they built something good!

Shazzon Bradley is a good example of doing just that. Raised in an unbearably abusive home, he ran away at age nine, sleeping anywhere he could. At age 16, he witnessed a gang surround a man and stab him to death. The event shocked Shazzon, both the killing and how that man was a relentless fighter until his last breath.

Later, Shazzon learned that the man the gang killed was actually his own father! He took his guilty feelings (for not getting involved) and channeled those into a commitment to be a fighter himself.

He went from homeless to playing football at the University of Tennessee and was even drafted by the Green Bay Packers, though he didn't make the final cut. He then went into boxing and became a pro boxer, never losing a fight.

There are countless stories of people from every corner of the world who quietly rebuilt their lives after trauma. They created new habits to replace the old by focusing on moving forward rather than on only seeing their failure or limitations.

One curious thing about training to overcome trauma is that you inevitably become a teacher yourself. That is because there are always (and I mean always!) people around you who need to see you succeed. Your success not only motivates them to do the same, but you will have answers to their questions. And when you teach others, you learn twice.

 Now You Know:

Symptoms of trauma and stress may wax and wane over time. Press on. It will pass.

This is where your mission comes into play. It is often a natural extension of all that you have done to grow, to break free of trauma, to stop bad habits, and to reach your dreams.

Paul was himself a teacher and he taught his students:

Show yourself in all respects to be a model of good works,
and in your teaching show integrity, dignity (Titus 2:7 ESV).

You are doing just that when you teach others by your own example. You are a model of good works! Good job. Keep it up. And push away negative thoughts of anxiety about having people rely on you. You don't have to be an expert.

PRACTICAL STEPS WITH YOUR TRAINING

If you are battling trauma or overwhelmed with stress, learning something new in order to create new habits may be the last thing on your mind. Most likely, you'd probably prefer to hide from the world rather than dive into new things.

I get it. However, training is very important for your healing. This applies, even in tough times.

- **Going through a messy divorce?** Block off time for learning and creativity.
- **Lost your job?** It's the perfect time to learn new skills that will help with your job search or volunteer someplace where it can fill in a gap on your resume.
- **Laid up in bed from a sickness or accident?** Take online courses that help you with your current or next job.
- **Told again by friends and family that you are a failure?** Study, learn, and keep looking for answers, help, mentors, and opportunities (and better friends).
- **Wondering if the trauma will ever end?** The first three years after trauma can be the toughest, and symptoms can reappear decades later. Read biographies of people who recovered from tragedy. Seek inspiration.

Even though you feel like quitting, don't do it. Don't check out. Don't retreat. And don't slow down.

You may not get that job back, that relationship may not work out, and family may never encourage you—but that does not mean life is over!

PAUL THE TEACHER

Paul was a prodigy of Jewish teachings from early in his life. After his epiphany on the road to Damascus, he studied and restudied incessantly what he had learned, because now he had to teach it to others.

All this perfected his own mental abilities to handle the intellectual arguments as well as the spiritual challenges. The more he debated, the better he became. Some debates ended in riots, death threats, beatings, and a stoning. Paul never ran from an argument, for he knew that if you run from battle, you never learn to fight, and that builds no courage.

Paul grew stronger, his teaching more continuous. He wrote, "Day after day, in the temple courts and from house to house, they never stopped teaching and proclaiming the good news that Jesus is the Messiah" (Acts 5:42 NIV).

He taught his students, "All Scripture is inspired by God and profitable for teaching, for reproof, for correction, for training in righteousness; so that the man of God may be adequate, equipped for every good work" (2 Timothy 3:16-17 NIV).

Keep moving forward. Be so busy that you have no time to be sad or self-destructive. And remember:

1. Training leads to mastery;
2. Mastery leads to confidence;
3. Confidence strengthens your commitment to continue;
4. All this increases your wisdom. (See Proverbs 3:13-23)

Seek wisdom, "For wisdom is protection just as money is protection, but the advantage of knowledge is that wisdom preserves the lives of its possessors" (Ecclesiastes 7:12 NASB).

If you are dealing with depression, plan for more rest during your training because depression causes physical and psychological fatigue. Just give yourself more time. In fact, if you're in college, your institution will often make accommodations if you ask. This can include giving you more time to complete assignments, tutoring, and counseling support on campus.

Pace yourself. Be patient. You know what you want to do, so take the time to do it right. Don't rush or overextend yourself.

Slow and steady wins the race.

Chapter 16

Step #9—Eat Healthy

When I was visiting an archeological dig site in Israel, I happened to arrive just as the workers were sitting down for lunch. I was struck by the colorful array of fresh foods on a large platter. It included tomato, cucumbers, scallions, black olives, dates, figs, avocados, and on the side was a bowl of yogurt drizzled with olive oil, pistachios, and flatbread for dipping. The seasoning was simple salt and pepper.

Their meal was similar to what has been eaten for thousands of years in the eastern Mediterranean region. We have a good idea of a typical diet during Paul's lifetime because there is so much written in the Bible, Torah, and Mishna about the different types of food and its preparation.

Common fruits included grapes, pomegranates, dates, apples, olives, and figs. Chickpeas, fava beans, and lentils would have been on the menu as legumes. Wine, vinegar, and water were often referenced as drinks.

Additionally, stale bread was dipped in those liquids and in sauces from fish, lamb, and olive oil. Meats included lamb, sheep, and goat, while pork was forbidden in kosher diets. Fowl that made the Biblical list included partridge, pigeon, quail, dove, chicken, and eggs from each. Vinegar, salting, or drying in the sun were used to preserve food.

In the book of Daniel (1:3–16 NLT), the King ordered his staff to "Select only strong, healthy, and good-looking young men," and feed them a selected daily diet of food and wine for three years. But Daniel asked instead to swap the King's prescribed diet for healthier foods. Daniel and his friends were healthier and better nourished than the young men who had been eating the food assigned by the king. A more recent study on Daniel's diet found fruits, vegetables, whole grains, legumes, nuts, and seeds (and no processed food) improved metabolism and cardiovascular health in men and women.[1]

In comparing today's foods to what was eaten back then, I would say the "Mediterranean diet" and the "healthy brain diets" are the closest to what Paul would likely have eaten.

Eating is not just an energy source for the body. What we eat, what we don't eat, when we eat, when we don't eat, and how we eat all have a profound effect on the brain's efficiency, our thinking, our moods, and our physical health.

Eating healthy is vital in your recovery from trauma and for living life to the fullest.

 Now You Know:

Living each day with purpose (including eating for health) unites healthy attitudes with healing beliefs, emotions, and actions.

THE NEED FOR HEALTHY EATING

Countless books, articles, and websites tout their diets and supplements as the best, but I think what Paul ate was good not only for the body but also for the brain.

And that is what we need to aim for as we work to stay healthy and recover from trauma and stress.

But have you noticed what we typically crave when we are anxious, depressed, or worried? Usually it's foods high in sugar, fat, and carbs. Depressed or anxious friends might confess to you how they ate an entire container of ice cream, box of cookies, bag of chips, or bottle of wine in one sitting.

These foods don't help. They actually contribute to cognitive slow down (decreased attention, comprehension, focus, and memory). What's more, snacks that are ultraprocessed to extend shelf life or shorten food preparation time actually decrease your life span.[2]

Follow all this with the normal low-exercise lifestyle, and you can see how the problems compound themselves.

Also, chronic stress and trauma already negatively affect the brain (and then your body), so eating unhealthy foods will only worsen your symptoms. But healthy eating, combined with exercise and good sleep, will help keep stress in check.

Healthy eating is absolutely fundamental on your journey to health.

10 HEALTHY EATING TIPS

Here are 10 tips or suggestions for eating healthy. Though these would certainly count as common-sense eating, they still need to be considered and then adapted into your routine.

Tip #1—To feed your brain: Your brain likes dark green vegetables, fresh fruit, fish proteins, and whole grains, but it does not like sugars, processed foods, and chemicals (such as growth hormones, insecticides, pesticides, and herbicides).

Tip #2—To fight depression: Foods and supplements with vitamin D and omega-3 fat (fish oil) have been found to help decrease levels of depression.

Tip #3—To decrease anxiety: Foods that help decrease anxiety include asparagus, avocado, vitamin C, antioxidants[3] (berries, fruit, and kale), seeds/nuts containing magnesium associated with improving serotonin levels associated with sleep and mood regulation (such as almonds), yogurt (fermented foods containing probiotics),[4] and drinking cocoa before a stressful event (lowers blood pressure, improves blood flow, and hastens post-stress recovery).[5]

Tip #4—To boost antioxidant levels: Antioxidants counter oxidative stress[6] on the brain. Foods with antioxidants include lettuce, broccoli, cauliflower, cabbage, sauerkraut, and Brussels sprouts and foods that are high in carotenoids (like tomatoes, carrots, yams/sweet potatoes, squash, kale, and spinach).[7]

Tip #5—To decrease stress: Blueberries reduce oxidative stress and inflammation in the brain, and restore balance to neurotransmitters in animals that have been subjected to traumatic stress.[8] Include foods like tea, dark grapes, apples, and cocoa.

Tip #6—To boost brain function: Coffee has positive effects on brain function. Other benefits include reduced heart disease, metabolic disorders like diabetes, and neurological problems impacting mental health and cognitive decline. A couple of cups of coffee is the optimal range, and not too close to bedtime.

Tip #7—To help your gut: Gut bacteria have been found to affect mood, neuropsychiatric conditions, inflammation, and wounds, and have been studied in relation to autism, Alzheimer's disease, manufacturing serotonin, and the modulation of anxiety.[9,10] A course of strong antibiotics can wipe out good gut bacteria, so adding more probiotics after a sickness that required antibiotics is usually necessary.

Tip #8—To stay hydrated: Dehydration results in changes in brain volume. When dehydrated, the brain requires more effort (thus consuming more energy) to achieve optimal performance. Drinking water (about fifteen cups a day for men, about eleven cups a day for women) is essential for keeping your brain and body at peak levels. Alcohol is a dehydrator, so consume it in moderation and drink the same amount of water.

Tip #9—To reduce inflammation: Polyphenols are compounds found in plant-based foods (such as red and pink fruit, walnuts, olive oil, green and yellow vegetables, and many berries such as strawberries and raspberries). Polyphenols help decrease inflammation in your body.[11]

Tip #10—To plan your meals: The Mediterranean diet has also been linked with a reduction in depression symptoms[12] and improved cognitive performance.[13] There are many good books available that describe the meal plans and recipes for "brain diets" and "Mediterranean diets." Choose one, work through it, and make it a habit.

When you are stressed, you are already at risk of neglecting your own health needs. That's why deciding in advance what you will eat and drink will prove to be incredibly helpful.

They always say that prior planning prevents poor performance, and that is especially true when it comes to eating healthy.

HEALTHY EATING HABITS

In addition to eating healthy foods, it is also important that you slow down and enjoy your meals with family and friends. That may sound like a cliché, but if you are battling trauma and chronic stress, eating with other people is extra important.

Why is eating with family and friends so important? Because building relationships during mealtime gives you the opportunity to grow emotionally and spiritually, and improve your mental and spiritual well-being.

If you haven't already, make mealtime a time to enjoy food and enjoy the company around the table.

Slowing down is also good for your body. It helps to relax your body, it aids digestion, and it contributes to your overall health.

A few rules that support this quality time together include:

- Turn off the TV or computer;
- No texting or cell phones at the table;
- Listen to what others are saying;
- Don't talk about work;
- Try to laugh at something;
- Be thankful;
- Tell a good story;
- Compliment each other (no criticism);
- Be positive, encouraging, and kind.

Multitasking is fine sometimes, just don't bring it to the table. Family members especially want to be valued and listened to, and that strengthens your family. It builds psychological confidence and helps everyone handle stress a little bit better.

This is not a trivial matter. Eating together at the table really does make a positive impact.

> So then, my brothers and sisters, when you gather to eat, you should all eat together (1 Corinthians 11:33 NIV).

> And day by day, attending the temple together and breaking bread in their homes, they received their food with glad and generous hearts (Acts 4:26 ESV).

Eating was more than just consuming food for Paul. It was a time to reflect on gratitude and faith:

> So whether you eat or drink, or whatever you do, do it all for the glory of God (1 Corinthians 10:31).

When we eat together, we are sending the message that we are interested in other people. We show empathy rather than judgment by simply being at the same table. It's kind, calming, and good for each one of us.

I believe that's why Jesus got such a reaction when He mixed things up and ate at the table with the "wrong" people. Imagine this:

> And as he reclined at the table in his house, many tax collectors and sinners were reclining with Jesus and his disciples, for there were many who followed him. And the scribes of the Pharisees, when they saw that he was eating with sinners and tax collectors, said to his disciples, "Why does he eat with tax collectors and sinners?" And when Jesus heard it, he said to them, "Those who are well have no need of a physician, but those who are sick. I came not to call the righteous, but sinners" (Matthew 9:10–13 ESV).

Jesus' most important meal was the final Passover when He gathered His disciples and described the sacrifice He was about to make. This Last Supper was so centrally important that it is remembered billions of times through the centuries in Christian religious services.

Make it a habit to enjoy your food and enjoy those around the table with you. That is simply good for your health!

 Now You Know:

Late meals and nighttime snacks can throw off your morning blood sugar levels, giving you the uneasy physical sensation in the morning that feels like "anxiety."

HOW FASTING BENEFITS YOUR HEALTH

I like to think of fasting as a purposeful choice. It's an opportunity to establish healthy eating habits, take even more control over stress and trauma, and build valuable spiritual strength.

Fasting is the act of eliminating or reducing your intake of certain foods and drinks for a set period. Fasting can be a complete limit of any food or removal of certain foods from your diet. It may range from extending the time between meals or going days without food.

Fasting that is starvation (e.g., anorexia or bulimia) is both physically and mentally unhealthy. Also, fasting should be planned, not passive inaction, such as when you are too tired, depressed, or stressed to eat.

As it relates to helping your body overcome the negative effects of stress and trauma, fasting has proven itself to be effective in ways that may surprise you. Consider the following:

- One study reported that women who fasted more than 13 hours overnight had a 36 percent lower chance of developing breast cancer than those who fasted less than 13 hours.[14]
- Intermittent fasting (total fasting 12 to 24 hours between meals on occasion or reducing caloric intake dramatically two days per week) has been associated with increased stress resistance in the brain and improved cognitive function.[15]
- Intermittent fasting reduces inflammation and helps you lose weight.[16,17]
- Intermittent fasting improves blood pressure, reduces LDL (bad cholesterol) by as much as 25 percent, and reduces triglycerides by as much as 32 percent from alternate day fasting for eight weeks.[18]

Fasting also increases your self-discipline by helping you gain control over cravings, which builds your mental strength. As you already know, when under stress, your body typically craves foods that only make things worse (i.e., sugars, carbs, etc.).

Cravings can override reason very quickly, but when you train your mind and body with fasting, you will be amazed at how much more self-control you have toward food. In fact, if you know you have a "weak spot" for comfort food, such as that extra-cheese pizza or a double chocolate cake, then you have found what you should fast.

When you fast, you break the power of junk food in your life. You will be stronger for doing so.

You see, foods you crave for comfort are connected to your internal reward system. From your brain to your stomach, all the pleasure, taste, comfort, soothing, and enjoyment are woven into your body. But you can cut the control chords by fasting.

What's more, fasting is beneficial because it helps strengthen your spiritual connections. Paul fasted for three days in the beginning of his spiritual awakening (Acts 9:9). Moses fasted for 40 days and nights (Exodus 34:28), as did Elijah (1 Kings 19:8) and Jesus (Matthew 4:1–2). These prolonged fasts were associated with a spiritual awakening. I do not recommend a 40-day fast from all foods. Your body will not tolerate it. However, even short-term fasting can be a part of your connection with a powerful spiritual experience.

Fasting is a catalyst for spiritual cleansing. This conscious choice to control physical pleasure strengthens your spirit over the temptations of the body. The intense focus required for a fast, accompanied by prayer and reflection, opens a spiritual connection with God.

I have found fasting to be especially effective when I am emotionally struggling.

Lastly, you don't have to head into the desert or mountains to fast. You can retain personal solitude by not drawing attention to your fasting at work, at home, in private, or even in public.

It is far more meaningful to fast in humility. Maintain your focus on self-control, patience, humility, endurance, and spiritual strength for a season.

It's good for your health.

PAUL WAS A MENTOR

From a Roman jail awaiting his execution, Paul wrote his final letters to Timothy. This last guidance from mentor to pupil was honest, tender, and optimistic. As Paul recalled his own persecutions, he warned Timothy that he too would be tested, but encouraged Timothy to stay the course.

He wrote, "I give you this charge: Preach the word; be prepared in season and out of season; correct, rebuke and encourage—with great patience and careful instruction. For the time will come when people will not put up with sound doctrine. Instead, to suit their own desires, they will gather around them a great number of teachers to say what their itching ears want to hear. They will turn their ears away from the truth and turn aside to myths. But you, keep your head in all situations, endure hardship, do the work of an evangelist, discharge all the duties of your ministry" (2 Timothy 4:1-5 NIV).

SET YOURSELF UP FOR GOOD HEALTH

When it comes right down to it, health is a choice. It's a target that you aim toward. You plan on it and by doing so, you set yourself up for success.

During my Navy service, some of my active-duty training time was assigned to work with Navy SEAL teams. When I visited their galley (cafeteria), I noticed right away how vastly different their food selection was from what I've seen at any other military bases, including the dining area at Walter Reed National Military Medical Center, military bases in Iraq and Afghanistan, or on aircraft carriers.

Most military cafeterias include a salad bar, perhaps a few cooking stations, sandwich selections, some healthy foods, and a wide range of the usual hamburgers, pizza, processed foods, sodas, etc. Many bases have a McDonalds, Pizza Hut, or other fast-food options.

Not so with the SEALs. Their food stations were labeled for their function, like "Protein" and "Antioxidants." The protein options included salmon, chicken breast, and lean red meats. Nothing deep fried. Fresh fruits, nuts, berries, and green salads were abundant. You could even get a healthy fruit smoothie and a protein bar to go. There was no white sugar to be found anywhere. And there was access to water everywhere to stay well hydrated when working out.

Warriors eat to keep their brains and bodies in shape during the intense demands of training. Take a look at *The Special Operations Forces Nutrition Guide*[19] for a description of nutritional habits to support a physically and mentally demanding routine. Think of it as a guide for fueling your fight against operational stress.

Not only did the intentionality of the good food choices strike me, but it was the fact that there were no other options. They were setting themselves up for success.

At home, if your fridge, freezer, or pantry includes foods you know you shouldn't be eating, then the odds are high that you will want to eat them someday. Perhaps when you are under stress or feeling down, those foods will look extra appealing.

The answer is to get rid of it. Then restock your shelves with foods that keep your health on course.

You know that the foods you eat will either strengthen or weaken your brain, body, emotions, and spirit. Set yourself up for good health by limiting your options to only the good options. That's what you want, anyway!

Rest assured that as your diet and health improve, you will see gains in your attention, concentration, memory, a better stress response, and you will break free of the mental fog. Even if it takes you several months or a year to set things in place, it's time well spent.

It's your health we are talking about!

Chapter 17

Step #10—Learn to Relax

With my four-year-old granddaughter's cancer, every day brought another punch in the gut of bad news. It was a long and brutal road: diagnosis, consultations, chemotherapy, side effects of chemo, weight loss, surgery, postsurgical complications, infections, delaying chemo until the infections cleared up, more chemo, vomiting, more weight loss, dehydration, kidney problems, more surgery, more complications, curled up for hours on the couch barely moving, praying for good news, and more. The cycle did not ever seem to end.

Through all of this, I watched my daughter and son-in-law striving to be optimistic, but every day strained their emotions, hope, faith, and resources as they juggled time with work, family, and their three-year-old son. How do you keep life "normal" in that?

They climbed their giant mountain daily, and each time they reached what they thought was the peak, they saw even higher mountains before them continuing upward.

As you know, trauma is a tenacious monster. It doesn't easily release its grip. And all the while, life's difficulties maintain their full assault on your brain, body, and soul.

THE NEED FOR RELAXATION

You can't control every cause of stress in your life, but you can control your physical and mental response to those stresses. That is where relaxation comes in. It is your on/off switch for stress.

And you get to use that switch. It's under your control.

Stress usually gives you the "pedal to the metal" feeling, zaps your energy, causes inflammation, elevates your heart rate and blood pressure, weakens your immune system, ruins sleep, and causes toxins to build up in your body. On the mental side of things, stress causes flashbacks, nightmares, anxiety, worry, fear, lack of peace, and trouble concentrating.

This is no news flash. Scientists have done countless studies over the years on humans and animals, only to prove what everyone knows—that stress is bad for every part of your body.

You need to take your foot off the gas and slow things down. You need to regain control.

12 TIPS FOR RELAXATION

To regain control, you first need to learn how to relax. These 12 tips may seem obvious, but I'm spelling them out because most people need the reminders:

Tip #1—Unpack your day a little: You don't have to pack every moment of the day with something to do. Society may be pressuring you to make sure your kids' days are filled with school, sports, tutoring, lessons, and extracurricular activities from age three to 18, but you don't have to. This workaholic obsession is not a very bright future. If you are doing the same to yourself, packing every waking moment with something to do, then you really need to slow down. Unpack a bit, even just a little. Give yourself a little room to breathe.

Tip #2—Take time to recharge: Relaxation is not the same as sleep. Sleep is good, and it restores your brain and body to health. Relaxation, however, is the ability to set aside your work and your worries and give yourself a break during a busy day so you can recharge. Productivity is great, but burnout will nullify your productivity. Take a breather. Pause, recharge, and then get back out there.

Tip #3—Actually take a vacation: If you go on a vacation, don't bring your work with you. Not only does your family want to be with you, but your mind and body need a vacation as well. I used to pretend I was relaxing when I went on vacation with the family, but I was nonstop taking calls, emailing, texting, and planning. It hurt me, and it hurt my wife and daughter. You would think my headaches, insomnia, depression, or impatience would have been a clue. I should have actually taken a vacation when I had the chance. So the next time you go on vacation, don't pretend. Do it for real!

Tip #4—Make your alone time profitable: Isolation is not relaxation. Isolation is withdrawing to avoid contact with others because of social anxiety, panic, or extreme distress. It's staying in bed all day with the shades drawn, feeling miserable, and wallowing in self-pity. That does not count as profitable alone time. Instead, when you are alone with your thoughts, seek peace and quiet, away from the bombardment of a hyperstimulating world. That is relaxing, and it's profitable.

Tip #5—Don't waste your relaxation time: If you are relaxing, don't fill your time with news, TV, movies, blogs, or content that is negative, discouraging, or simply not good for you. That also includes alcohol, drugs, work email, and social media browsing. You should avoid all of that. If you are trying to relax, let it be good and true relaxation.

Tip #6—Talk nice to yourself: Beating yourself up is not relaxing. You know that, but it's easy to fall into that trap when you slow down. That's because your mind is quick to fill the silence with outstanding bills, broken relationships, unproductive meetings, and idle gossip. This only makes things worse, so turn it off. Remember your successes, and your hopes. It's more relaxing and it's good for your self-esteem.

Tip #7—Do what you want to do: Go play with your children. Take a walk with someone you care about. Listen to others talk. Enjoy your hobby. Laugh at, jokes, or shows. Enjoy the moment. Take a nap in a hammock. Curl up with a cup of tea and your favorite book. Smell the flowers. Plant a tree. Whatever it is you enjoy that is really relaxing, do it. Do just what you want to do.

Tip #8—Unplug: Turn off all technology. Shut off all sounds, images, and words. Even if it's only for a few minutes, purposefully go unplugged. Sit still. Breathe. Let your concentration be uninterrupted.

Tip #9—Start your day calmly: Start the day relaxed. Plan for soothing thoughts as the first thing when you awaken. Set your alarm 10 minutes early to give yourself time to start relaxed. Jumping up and rushing into your day is not restful or calm! Have soothing music on your phone to play, stretch out for a few minutes, read a motivating book, list things you are grateful for, read a verse or passage of scripture, or do some breathing exercises. Make your morning routine one that extends calm as you move into your day.

Tip #10—Breathe deeply: In the morning, before going to bed, or any time during the day, deep breathing is good for you. The old adage of "count to 10 before you reply" was good advice. Breathing deeply will slow down a racing heart. In tense situations, when under stress, take a minute to breathe. It will help.

Tip #11—Stretch your legs: If at work, take a break when you can, even if just to stand up and stretch. And when it is break time, take a real break. Walk for five minutes. Just don't keep working at your desk. Your body, mind, blood circulation, and concentration will benefit you every time you stretch your legs.

Tip #12—Unwind at the end of the day: Make time to unwind from your own daily pressures. After work, exercise, take your dog for a walk, walk yourself, or do an enjoyable outside project. A simple walk in the woods for 20 minutes has a significant impact on physically calming you down.[1] Even sitting still at home after work will help you unwind. You decide what is relaxing for you, and then do it each day.

The whole point of relaxing is to actually relax, catch your breath, and clear your head. It's to refresh and renew your mind, body, mission, and energy. When you do relax, all the problems that burden you have a way of shifting or changing. You not only have more hope and peace, but also start to see solutions.

By relaxing, you regain control in every area, and staying in control is excellent for your health.

 Now You Know:

There is more to relaxing than just not working. It has a real purpose. It is a time to experience gratitude, joy, and appreciate what is around you.

DID PAUL EVER RELAX?

Paul was a learner, reader, teacher, preacher, leader, writer, debater, prisoner, traveler, and tent maker. His responsibilities were enormous, but even Paul took a break once in a while. He even told others to join him in rest: "And to you who are troubled, rest with us" (2 Thessalonians 1:7 KJB).

He encouraged this "rest" for the Thessalonians, who themselves were intensely persecuted. Paul's use of "rest" is best understood in the original Greek word "anesis" meaning relief, lessening, or stopping stress. In the language of ancient Greece, it described releasing the pressure of the string on an archer's bow. In modern medicine, we would say "the symptoms are in remission."

> There remains, then, a Sabbath-rest for the people of God; for anyone who enters God's rest also rests from their works, just as God did from his. Let us, therefore, make every effort to enter into that that rest . . . (Hebrews 4:9-11).

Rest brings renewal of the mind and spirit. Paul understood that as well: "Therefore, we do not lose heart. Though outwardly we are wasting away, yet inwardly we are being renewed day by day" (2 Corinthians 4:16 NIV).

Paul knew he did not have to carry every burden on his own. He relaxed and let it go.

RELAX WITH MEDITATION

Meditation is not only an excellent way to relax, it is especially effective when dealing with stress and trauma. Meditation is intentionally eliminating all distractions in your environment and focusing your mind. This means clearing away all the cluttering thoughts, behaviors, and emotions while concentrating on a calming, motivating, positive message.

There is a process to meditation. Here is my seven-step process for healthy meditation:

Step #1—Select a place to sit by yourself. "When you pray, go into your room, close the door, and pray to your Father" (Matthew 6:6 NIV).

Step #2—Seek silence. Play soft music or white noise to mask interferences and help you concentrate. Turn off any potential distractions. "The wisest thing you can do is to keep quiet" (Job 13:5 CEV).

Step #3—Close your eyes. Concentrate on the calm. "He hushed the storm to silence and the waves of the sea were stilled. They rejoiced that the sea grew calm, that God brought them to the harbor they longed for " (Psalm 107:29–30 NABRE).

Step #4—Breathe slowly. Inhale for four seconds, hold for four seconds, exhale for four, and hold for four (this is "box breathing"). Do this for a few minutes. Exhale stress and inhale new life. "I will cause breath to enter you, and you will come to life" (Ezekiel 37:5 BSB).

Step #5—Focus on relaxing muscle groups. Start with your toes and work your way up to your face. Tense each muscle group for 10 seconds, then relax. Take a few slow deep breaths. Concentrate on the feeling of relaxation. ". . . from whom the whole body, being fitted and held together by what every joint supplies, according to the proper working of each individual part, causes the growth of the body for the building up of itself in love" (Ephesians 4:16 NASB).

Step #6—Think about a selected word or phrase. Keep it simple, positive, and affirming. Listen to it, think about it, repeat it many times. If negative thoughts try to interfere, push them out right away with your positive phrase. "Practice these things, immerse yourself in them" (1 Timothy 4:15 ESV).

Step #7—Meditate for 10 to 20 minutes. Dwell on your positive message, then gradually pull yourself out from your meditation, being re-aware of the world around you, ". . . prepare your minds for action" (1 Peter 1:13 NLT).

Then continue your day, maintaining the attitude/phrase you focused on during your meditation.

You may be wondering what you should meditate on. It will change over time, but I always recommend a word or phrase that:

- Keeps you focused and in control;
- Is valuable, helpful, and beneficial to you;
- Is trustworthy.

A friend of mine, a Navy SEAL veteran, said that he recites Psalm 23 when he is running. That's a lot of repetition! He said, "Every time I say it, I get something different out of it, and I am strengthened even more." That was his meditational phrase that kept him in control, it made him stronger, and it was from a reliable source.

I have had clients who are worried that if they mediate and get quiet their bad thoughts will take control. Actually, the opposite is true. Because meditation is purposeful focus, you remain in control. You own it, and can fill the time with thoughts of beauty, peace, hope, and faith. Focused meditation shines light in the shadows and builds your strength to fight back. As you practice, your trust will grow. I like what Judges 6:23 (NIV) says: "Peace! Do not be afraid. You are not going to die."

By the way, you have probably been meditating for years without knowing it. However, your meditation may have involved the repetition of destructive messages: "I am a failure," "I will never shake this problem," etc. Replace those toxic phrases with healthy reflections!

MEDITATE WITH PRAYER

Prayer is the ultimate meditation. As you grow in your ability to meditate, you will bring those calming skills into moments of crisis. King David from the Bible was great at that. Here are his own words:

> The enemy pursues me,
> he crushes me to the ground;
> he makes me dwell in the darkness
> like those long dead.
> So my spirit grows faint within me;
> my heart within me is dismayed.
> I remember the days of long ago;
> I meditate on all your works
> and consider what your hands have done.
> (Psalm 143:3–5 NIV)

Prayer requires many of the elements included in meditation, such as centering your mind on the moment, clearing away unessential distractions, and focusing on a specific message. And as you pray, your words can be quiet contemplation or spoken out loud. You can also pray alone or in a group.

There are four types of prayer:

1. **Adoration**: praising, reading, and learning about God
2. **Contrition**: admitting your errors and asking forgiveness
3. **Petition**: requesting favor/healing/strength on behalf of yourself or someone else
4. **Gratitude**: listing the many things you are thankful for

 Now You Know:

True prayer is genuine, humble, and honest.

Prayer builds your faith and hope. Even when the world seems to be crashing around you, prayer is your ally. Call it up as your reinforcements. You don't have to have the quiet, candle-lit room, with soft celestial music. Pray wherever you are, clearing your mind from the torments of the moment.

One word of caution about prayer: People often get frustrated with prayer because they don't get their prayers answered in the direction or time they wanted. But prayer does not mean you will always get what you want when you want it. I believe that all prayers do get answered, but sometimes the answer is "yes," sometimes "no," and sometimes "not yet."

I know how frustrating the answer "not yet" can be. But we have no power over all the world. However, we do have the power to control our own choices, minds, decisions, and dreams. Pray to understand, not to demand.

It all goes back to what we think about. Paul gave very clear instructions on what we should think about, which also applies to our meditation and prayers:

> Finally, brothers and sisters, whatever is true, whatever is noble, whatever is right, whatever is pure, whatever is lovely, whatever is admirable—if anything is excellent or praiseworthy—think about such things. Whatever you have learned or received or heard from me, or seen in me—put it into practice. And the God of peace will be with you (Philippians 4:8–9 NIV).

Meditative prayers are prayers that you repeat often. These also will change over time. My clients have told me that their meditative prayers helped them focus and relax at the same time. Asking God for help affirms their own desire to let go and not carry the weight of stress or pressure. Here are a few of their short meditative prayers:

- "Help me to forgive others."
- "Help me forgive myself."
- "Show me the way."
- "Help me to understand."
- "I know you love me."
- "This is for my good."
- "Thank you."

Find the words that are right for you, then meditate on them as you pray throughout the day.

Instead of relaxing when they have the chance, many people worry instead. Worry grips them, tying them up in knots, always wondering if what they envisioned will come to pass. But though the worry hardly ever comes to pass, they keep on doing it.

It's habitual, it's bad, and all it does is add anxiety and pressure to our life, but it can be stopped.

For your sake, it must be stopped.

Paul knew worry was useless and even dangerous. His profoundly simple message was:

> Do not worry about anything, but in everything by prayer and supplication with thanksgiving let your requests be made known to God (Philippians 4:6 NRSV).

The best remedy against worry is prayer.

RELAX WITH MINDFULNESS

While meditation concentrates your attention on a focused message separate from distractions of the moment, mindfulness brings you entirely into the moment. You are fully alive and fully aware of every sound, sight, smell, feeling, and thought. There is no past or future, only the now.

Here is an example of how that works and how that can be helpful: Years ago, a paramedic told me about his certification for cave diving. The training was intense. He had to navigate a confusing underwater labyrinth in complete darkness while searching for a rope that would guide him out. The only light was a small headlamp. This required controlled breathing, mental focus, and nerves that remained calm. During his test, his light went out! His heart began to race, but he forced himself to stay calm. His mindfulness training kicked in, which prevented panic. He found the rope in complete darkness, and followed it out.

Obviously, not every situation is as desperate as that, but in your own moments, mindfulness will give you the advantage you need. It is a practiced habit that will come back to you whenever you need it.

There are four parts to preparing a mindfulness habit:

Part #1—Clear the clutter. Concentrate on only what is essential in that moment. Imagine putting nonessential issues into boxes on the shelf to be addressed later.

Part #2—Be here and only here. To be in the moment, focus on every sight, sound, smell, taste and touch. Ignore every distracting thought of the past and future. The past and future do not belong in your full attention to now.

Part #3—Fight the triggers. Your emotions are real and are not to be ignored. If you are in a situation that you think may "trigger" you, don't retreat. Prepare and strengthen yourself instead. Focus on the moment, not the past.

Part #4—Practice. Rehearse mindfulness in the easy times, so you are ready for the tough times. Practice with mild to moderate stresses to increase your confidence. Always keep practicing. Try mindfulness while doing a common task such as preparing a meal, taking a walk or just sitting still, practice being fully in the moment, focusing on each of your senses. This builds the self-control you will need when anxious memories try to interfere.

I have seen mindfulness at work in people's lives, and it is always encouraging. The benefits of mindfulness make the effort well worth it. Here are a few of the many benefits that you can enjoy:

- Mindfulness saves you energy.
- Mindfulness makes you more perceptive.
- Mindfulness fights depression.
- Mindfulness reduces the perception of pain.
- Mindfulness fights impulsivity.
- Mindfulness increases awareness of wrong thoughts and then calls up the tools to remove them.
- Mindfulness makes you more compassionate.

Paul really gave us great insight into mindfulness when he wrote:

All bitterness, fury, anger, shouting, and reviling must be removed from you, along with all malice. Be kind to one another, compassionate, forgiving one another as God has forgiven you in Christ. (Ephesians 4:32 NABRE).

When you control your mind, you control your danger. That is really mindfulness at work.

PAUL KEPT NO SECRETS

Time and time again, Paul spoke about his past and present troubles. His trauma-fighting attitudes were acquired through experience, strengthened through repetition, and understood through humility.

He focused on the goodness of God, supported with an attitude of prayer to calm any anxiety. He wrote, "Be anxious for nothing, but in everything by prayer and supplication with thanksgiving let your requests be made known to God" (Philippians 4:6 NKJB).

I have witnessed people who were unable to turn off their stressful memories, and it really took a toll on them mentally, physically, and emotionally. But in every case, they were not practicing mindfulness.

Paul practiced mindfulness while on a boat in the middle of a storm. The boat was off course and the treacherous winter currents were threatening to smash them to the rocky shores. The tackle and supplies were thrown overboard to lighten the load and save the ship. No one could eat or sleep. Roman soldiers panicked and attempted to escape by a lifeboat, but Paul spoke up and got the crew to focus on survival rather than escape. Paul remained mindful of trust, not panic. He even told all aboard the ship, "Keep up your courage" (Acts 27:25 NASB).

Everyone on board the sinking ship survived, thanks to Paul's mindfulness. He kept them focused when nobody else could.

Mindfulness is both an excellent defense as well as a great offense. The more you make it part of you, the stronger and healthier you will be.

IF YOU ARE FIGHTING PTSD

Will meditation, prayer, and mindfulness cure PTSD? These do not erase trauma history, but they help keep the past in the past, allowing you to safely process memories in the present.

As you build meditation, prayer, and mindfulness skills, you may even discover new memories that alter your entire reaction to a past problem. A few real examples include:

- The Marine who blamed himself for his buddy's death, but when he more accurately remembered the combat scene, he realized there was no possible way he could have prevented his the death. This revelation allowed him to release his false guilt.
- The dad who beat himself up every day for his young son being hit by a car finally put the facts together and understood that the injuries could not have been prevented by anything he did.
- The woman living for years with guilt that she was the cause of the assault against her as a student finally understood her actions did not provoke the attack. She let go of her punitive shame.

Our minds tend to wander about half the time, and that is where anxious thoughts can sneak in. Meditation, prayer, and mindfulness improve our ability to focus attention and gain control over our thoughts.

Practicing meditation, prayer, and mindfulness does not mean a traumatic memory will never reappear. They have their own established memory connectomes in your brain. With time, you will unlearn the anxious and create new calm brain paths.

Over time, the healthy connections will only get stronger.

- If you are headed to a potentially stressful event, try meditation before you go, and practice mindfulness while you are there. "I am safe. I can do this."
- If a trigger event happens, stay in the moment, remind yourself you are OK, and that the "trigger" was merely a reminder, not the real trauma. "I am safe."
- If you are in a stressful conversation, it's OK to excuse yourself, take a break, walk away from the stressing conversation, go to a quieter area, and take a few calming breaths. Remind yourself—that was then, this is now. Past and present are only connected if you connect them. You are in control. Then go back into the room or conversation, even if for a brief time, so you can prove you can be a victor.

Keep practicing.

✳ ✳ ✳

All of these life skills—meditation, prayer, and mindfulness—improve with practice.

Keep at it. Your health deserves it!

Conclusion

Everyone has experienced trauma. Some worse than others, but the internal battles speak of the continual need for freedom and healing.

Always remember: trauma does not own you. You can walk free.

As you travel on your journey to health and freedom from trauma, here is a recap of the 10 steps to *getting* and *staying* healthy:

Step #1—Actively build your own resilience: Resilience is within you. Choose to be strong, be disciplined at all times, use solitude to benefit you, be humble, and set goals of where you want to go.

Step #2—Arm your resistance: You've got to resist the trauma and stress. Choose to be courageous, always fight, connect with your community, and remain vigilant at all times.

Step #3—Embrace your recovery: You can recover! Choose to keep hold of hope, walk into your healing, leave self-blame alone, and forgive everyone—yourself included.

Step #4—Accept your renewal: This is daily improvement. Choose to walk by faith, keep your trust, give and live with grace, and find the mission that excites you.

Step #5—Get fit: Fitness is supposed to be a gradual, lifelong process. Start now, keep at it, and you can enjoy it for the rest of your life.

Step #6—Strengthen your attitude: Your attitude is your habit of thoughts. So choose wisely the habits you want, and then become the person you want to be.

Step #7—Get enough sleep: Sleep is a vital part of your health, so do what it takes to establish routines that get you a good night's sleep.

Step #8—Train yourself: The journey to becoming the best version of yourself always includes training. It means getting better, little by little.

Step #9—Eat healthy: Because your body wins or loses by what you put in your mouth, take action to give your body what it needs to sustain the long life you want.

Step #10—Learn to relax: Relaxation is necessary for your body, from head to toe. Learn to relax, meditate, pray, and be mindful.

Paul has been our example through trauma, and he persevered through years of constant, additional, and increasing trauma. It was not a one-time event for him, but rather a way of life!

Near the end of his life (right before he was beheaded), he wrote some of the most compelling, most challenging words of all time:

> I have fought the good fight, I have finished the race, I have kept the faith (2 Timothy 4:7 NIV).

Those are words to live by!

There were those who had abandoned and betrayed Paul along his journey, but he wrote to Timothy and told him not to allow any grudges to distract him. Distractions are just distractions.

Let go of what does not matter.

What's more, Paul also understood that the suffering done *to him* paled in comparison to the sacrifice accomplished *for him*. Paul dedicated his life to being worthy of the sacrifice of Jesus. He did not submit to depression. He celebrated with joy.

Like Paul, we are never alone. We are never lost.

When I hit my lowest point in life where I really did not care about living anymore, my family, friends, and wife saved me by believing in me and loving me. I did not deserve their love and grace, but they gave it anyway.

Your worst days can become the foundation for the best days of your life! That is true for me and for thousands of other people who have used these 10 steps to getting healthy and staying healthy.

You can build and rebuild your strength. You can arm yourself with courage and embrace hope. You can accept the faith, trust, grace, and mission given to you.

Be transformed by a renewing of your mind. And know that God's will for you is nothing less than the perfect version of yourself, healed and whole!

You can. You must. You will.

Acknowledgments

First and foremost, I must thank my family and friends, who were emotionally and spiritually supportive of me throughout this project. Their loyalty, candor, and prayers continue to lift me up. This includes my wife, Nanette, and daughter, Bevin and her family Dan, Thomasina, Luca, and Nico. Family friends include Tim Ryan, Dick Jewell, Mike DeVanney, Rob and Christine Ree, Devlin Robinson, and Greg and Jacqueline von Schleppenbach.

As I am no Biblical scholar, I am extremely grateful to those who provided ongoing scriptural guidance, including Rev. Kurt Jenkins, Rev. Drew Harvey, Tunch Ilkin, Rev. Dan Cummins, Jeff Cavins and Dale Killmeyer. Invaluable faith and faithful support over the years came from Rev. Patrick Conroy, Bishop David Zubik, Bishop David Bonnar, Jon Kolb (veteran Pittsburgh Steeler), Leo Wisniewski (veteran Baltimore and Indianapolis Colts), and the mighty men from my Bible study groups. Thank you for your instruction and prayers.

Joe Maroon, MD (neurosurgeon for the Pittsburgh Steelers) gave brilliant counsel on the neurology of stress. Excellent psychological research assistance was from my Navy colleagues/friends CDR Lloyd Davis, PhD and CDR Eric Potterat, PhD (veteran command psychologist for Navy Special Warfare and performance psychologist with the Los Angeles Dodgers).

Special thanks to those who were supportive of me through my military career and who taught me a great deal about trauma recovery: ADM Mike Mullen, ADM Jonathan Greenert, VADM Forest Faison, MD (former Navy Surgeon General), Vice ADM Mike Miller, Vice ADM Dirk Debbink, Captain Ben Bocuzzi (Navy), Colonel Geoffrey Grammer MD (Army), Colonel John Robinson USAF, Lew Knopp (NSW), Dave Williamson, MD (Founder and Director of the TBI/PTSD unit at Walter Reed National Military Medical Center at Bethesda), and psychologist Johanna Wolf. And thank you to Ryan Wakim MD psychiatrist and Chief Medical Officer for our program Fortis Future, treating veterans and first responders with PTSD.

Tip O'Neil famously said, "If you want a friend in Washington, get a dog," however, my experience disproves this as I am honored and humbled by the ongoing friendship from Representatives Gresham Barrett (SC), Jo Bonner (AL), Tom Cole (OK), Jeff Fortenberry (NE), Trent Franks (AZ), Mike Kelly (PA), and Guy Reschenthaler (PA), as well as Sarah Chamberlain, Mike Ingrao, Nate Nevalla, Mike D'Orazio, and Bob Cranmer.

For their enthusiastic support for this project, I am indebted to author Pete Early, Keith Burris (former editor of the Pittsburgh *Post Gazette* and *Toledo Blade*), Paul Kengor (author and professor at Grove City College), and Mary Glenn of Humanix Books. A special shout out to Brian Mast for his editing acumen.

Finally, to all my friends, patients, and clients over the years who taught me so much through their journey from trauma to renewal, thank you. Together, we continue to learn that we can, we must and we will.

Endnotes

CHAPTER 1

1   Paul, G. *Women and children first.* 2012.

CHAPTER 2

1   Parsaik AK, Ahlskog JE, Singer W, Gelfman R, Sheldon SH, Seime RJ, Craft JM, Staab JP, Kantor B, . . . Low, PA. Central hyperadrenergic state after lightning strike. *Clinical autonomic research: official journal of the Clinical Autonomic Research Society.* 2013; *23*(4), 169–73.

2   Cooper MA, Alcock J. Lightning injuries. *Medscape.* November 2017.

CHAPTER 3

1   Jackson SE, Kirschbaum C, Steptoe. A Hair cortisol and adiposity in a population-based sample of 2,527 men and women aged 54 to 87 years. *Obesity.* March 2017; 25 (3), 539–544.

2   Yehuda R, Bierer LM, Andrew R, Schmeidler J, Seckl JR. Enduring effects of severe developmental adversity, including nutritional deprivation, on cortisol metabolism in aging Holocaust survivors. *J Psychiatr Res.* 2009; 43, 877–83.

3   Dajani R, Hadfield K, Uum S, Greff M, Panter-Brick C. Hair cortisol concentrations in war-affected adolescents: A prospective intervention trial. *Psychoneurology.* 2018; 89, 138–46.

4   Kim YK, Maes M. The role of the cytokine network in psychological stress. *Acta Neuropsychiatrica.* 2013; 15, 148–55.

5   Reale M, Constantini E, D'Angelo C, et al. Network between Cytokines, Cortisol and Occupational Stress in Gas and Oilfield Workers. *Int. J. Mol. Sci.* 2020; 21, 1118.

6   Köhler CA, Freitas TH, Maes M, et al. Peripheral cytokine and chemokine alterations in depression: a meta-analysis of 82 studies. *Acta Psychiatr Scand.* 2017; 135(5): 373–87.

7   Wang Z, Young MR. PTSD, a Disorder with an Immunological Component. *Frontiers in immunology.* 2016; 7, 219.

8   Remch M, Laskaris Z, Flory J, Mora-McLaughlin C, Morabia A. Post traumatic stress disorder and cardiovascular diseases: a cohort study of men and women involved in cleaning the debris of the World Trade Center complex. *Circ Cardiovasc Qual Outcomes.* 2018; 11(7).

9   Cohen BE. Exploring posttraumatic stress disorder as a cardiovascular risk factor in women veterans. *JAMA Cardiol.* 2021; 6(6): 651–52.

CHAPTER 4

1   An Inventor's Seasoned Ideas. *The New York Times.* April 8, 1934.

CHAPTER 5

1   *Firefighter Fatalities in the United States in 2016.* US Fire Administration. FEMA. December 2017.

2   CIGNA U.S. Loneliness Index. MAY 2018.

3   Holt-Lunstad J. (2017) The Potential Public Health Relevance of Social Isolation and Loneliness: Prevalence, Epidemiology, and Risk Factors. *Public Policy & Aging Report.* 2017; 27(4), 127–30.

4   Lawrence, TE. (1935) *Seven Pillars of Wisdom.* Doubleday, Doran and Company. Original unpublished text in Oxford University collection 1922.

CHAPTER 6

1   Christensen AV, Juel K, Ekolm O, et al. Significantly increased risk of all-cause mortality among cardiac patients feeling lonely. *Heart.* January 2020; 106(2): 140–146.

2   Freedman SA, Gilad M, Ankri Y, Roziner I, Shalev AY. Social relationship satisfaction and PTSD: which is the chicken and which is the egg? *European journal of psychotraumatology.* December 2015.

3   Giles L. (2013) *Sun Tzu On the Art of War.* Abingdon, Oxon: Routledge. 2013.

CHAPTER 7

1   Aung San Suu Kyi. (1991) *Freedom from Fear and Other Writings.* London, UK: Penguin

2   Graham WF. (July 1964) A Time for Moral Courage. *Reader's Digest.* 49

3   Brooks P. (1886) "Going Up to Jerusalem." Twenty Sermons.

CHAPTER 8

1   Wilde, Oscar. (1893) *A Woman of No Importance.*

2   Wade NG, Hoyt, WT, Kidwell JEM, & Worthington, EL, Jr. Efficacy of psychotherapeutic interventions to promote forgiveness: A meta-analysis. *Journal of Consulting and Clinical Psychology.* 2014; *82*(1): 154–170.

CHAPTER 10

1   Pascal B. (1660) *Penseés* (Thoughts) VII (425).

2   Baetz ZM, Bowen R. Chronic pain and fatigue: associations with religion and spirituality. *Pain Res Manag.* 2008; 13, 383–88.

3   Barlas FM, Higgins WB, Pflieger JC, Diecker K. Health Related Behaviors Survey of Active Duty Military Personnel: Executive Summary (Department of Defense). 2013. Contract No. GS-23F-8182H.

4   Fontana A, Rosenheck RJ. Trauma, change in strength of religious faith, and mental health service use among veterans treated for PTSD. *Nerv Ment Dis.* September 2004; 192(9): 579–84.

5   Litz BT, Lebowitz L, Gray MJ, Nash WP. (2015) Adaptive Disclosure: A New Treatment for Military Trauma, Loss, and Moral Injury. New York, NY: Guilford Press, 2015.

6   Giordano GN, Lindstom M. Trust and health: testing the reverse causality hypothesis. *J Epidemiology and Community Health.* 7 (10).

CHAPTER 11

1   Kleiman EM, Adams LM, Kashdan TB, Riskind JH. Grateful individuals are not suicidal: Buffering risks associated with hopelessness and depressive symptoms. *Personality and Individual Differences.* 2013; 55(5): 595–99.

CHAPTER 12

1 Adlaf EW, Vaden RJ, Niver AJ, et al. Adult-born neurons modify excitatory synaptic transmission to existing neurons. *eLife*. eLife 2017;6:e19886.

2 Chatzi C, Zhang G, Hendricks WD, Chen Y, Schnell E, Goodman RH, Westbrook GL. Exercise-induced enhancement of synaptic function triggered by the inverse BAR protein, Mtss1L. *eLife*, 2019; 8.

3 Gomez-Pinilla F, Hillman C. The influence of exercise on cognitive abilities. *Comprehensive Physiology*. 2013; 3(1): 403–28.

4 Esteban-Cornejo I, Tejero-González CM, Martinez-Gomez D, del-Campo J, González-Galo A, Padilla-Moledo C, Sallis JF, Veiga OL. Independent and Combined Influence of the Components of Physical Fitness on Academic Performance in Youth. *The Journal of Pediatrics*. 2014.

5 Winter B, Breitenstein C, Mooren FC, et al. High impact running improves learning. Neurobiol Learn Mem. May 2007; 87(4): 597–09. Adler DA, Possemato K, Mavandadi S, et al. Psychiatric status and work performance of veterans of Operations Enduring Freedom and Iraqi Freedom. *Psychiatric Services*. 2011; 62: 39–46.

6 Hammer H, Batty GD. Association of body mass index and waist-to-hip ratio with brain structure UK Biobank study. *Neurology*. January 2019.

7 Caudate and putamen

8 Pallidum and nucleus accumbens

9 Kivipelto M, Ngandu T, Fratiglioni L, et al. Obesity and vascular risk factors at midlife and the risk of dementia and Alzheimer disease. *Arch Neurol*. 2005; 62(10): 1556–560.

10 Anderson E, Shivakumar G. Effects of exercise and physical activity on anxiety. *Frontiers in psychiatry*. 2013; 4, 27.

11 McDowell CP, Dishman RK, Gordon BR, Herring MP. Physical activity and anxiety: a systematic review and meta-analysis of prospective cohort studies. *Am J Preventive Medicine*. 2019; 57(4): 545–56.

12 Kandola AA, Osborn, DPJ, Stubbs B, et al. Individual and combined associations between cardiorespiratory fitness and grip

strength with common mental disorders: a prospective cohort study in the UK Biobank. *BMC Med.* 2020; 18, 303.

13 Hearing CM, Chang WC, Szuhany KL, et al. Physical exercise for treatment of mood disorders: A critical review. *Current behavioral neuroscience reports.* 2016; 3(4): 350–359.

14 Hegberg NJ, Hayes JP, Hayes SM. Exercise intervention in PTSD: A narrative review and rationale for implementation. *Frontiers in psychiatry.* 2019; 10: 133.

15 Matta P, Baul T, Plasencia BA, et al. Is sports participation protective of child mental health? *J Amer Acad Child Adol Psychiatry.* October 2019, 58(10).

16 Tandon PS, Zhou C, Johnson AM, Gonzalez ES, Kroshus E. Association of children's physical activity and screen time with mental health during the COVID-19 pandemic. *JAMA Netw Open.* 2021; 4(10): e2127892. doi:10.1001/jamanetworkopen.2021.27892.

17 Puzhko S, Aboushawareb SAE, Kudrina I, et al. Excess body weight as a predictor of response to treatment with antidepressants in patients with depressive disorder. *J Affect Disord.* 2020; 267, 153–70.

18 Duggal NA, Pollock RD, Lazarus NR, Harridge S, Lord JA. Major features of immunosenescence, including reduced thymic output, are ameliorated by high levels of physical activity in adulthood. *Aging Cell.* March 2018.

CHAPTER 13

1 Barnhofer T, Brennan K, Crane C, et al. A comparison of vulnerability factors in patients with persistent and remitting lifetime symptom course of depression. *Journal of affective disorders.* 2014; 152–154, 155–161. doi: 10.1016/j.jad.2013.09.001

2 Nicomedia Arrian. *The Enchiridion. AD 125.*

CHAPTER 14

1 Alonzo R, Hussain J, Stranges S, Anderson KK. Interplay between social media use, sleep quality, and mental health in youth: A systematic review. *Sleep Med Rev.* April 2021; 56, 101414. doi:10.1016/j.smrv.2020.101414.

2   Goldstein SJ, Gaston SA, McGrath JA, Jackson CL. Sleep health and serious psychological distress: A Nationally representative study of the united states among White, Black, and Hispanic/Latinx adults. *Nat Sci Sleep.* 2020; 12, 1091–1104.

3   Sabia S, Fayosse A, Dumurgier J. et al. Association of sleep duration in middle and old age with incidence of dementia. *Nat Commun.* 12, 2289.

4   Knutson KL, Spiegel K, Pemev P, Van Cauter E. The metabolic consequences of sleep deprivation. *Sleep Med Rev.* 2007; 11(3), 163–78.

5   Fernandez-Mendoza J, He F, Puzino K, et al. Insomnia with objective short sleep duration is associated with cognitive impairment: A first look at cardiometabolic contributors to brain health, *Sleep.* September 2020.

6   Wheaton AG, Shults RA, Chapman DP, et al. Drowsy driving and risk behaviors—10 states and Puerto Rico, 2011–2012. *Morbidity and Mortality Weekly Rep.* 2014; 63, 557–562.

7   Owens JM, Dingus TA, Guo F, Fang Y, Perez M, McClafferty J, Tefft BC. Prevalence of drowsy driving crashes: Estimates from a large-scale naturalistic driving study. *AAA Foundation for Traffic Safety.* 2018.

8   Borders A, Rothman, DJ, McAndrew LM. Sleep problems may mediate associations between rumination and PTSD and depressive symptoms among OIF/OEF veterans. *Psychological Trauma.* January 2015; 7(1): 76–84.

9   Kleim B, Wysokowsky J, Schmid N, Seifritz E, Rasch B. Effects of sleep after experimental trauma on intrusive emotional memories. *SLEEP.* 2016; 39(12): 2125

10 Davis CJ, Vanderheyden WM. Optogenetic sleep enhancement improves fear-associated memory processing following trauma exposure in rats. *Sci Rep.* 2020; 10(1).

CHAPTER 15

1   Adler DA, Possemato K, Mavandadi S, et al. Psychiatric status and work performance of veterans of Operations Enduring Freedom and Iraqi Freedom. *Psychiatric Services.* 2011; 62, 39–46.

2   Ramchand R, Rudavsky R, Grant S, Tanielian T, Jaycox L. Prevalence of, risk factors for, and consequences of posttraumatic stress disorder and other mental health problems in military populations deployed to Iraq and Afghanistan. *Curr Psychiatry Rep.* May 2015; 17(5): 37.

3   Goodman RD, Miller MD, West-Olatunji CA. Traumatic stress, socioeconomic status, and academic achievement among primary school students. *Psychological Trauma: Theory, Research, Practice, and Policy.* 2011.

4   Frugård Strøm I, Schultz, JH et al. School performance after experiencing trauma: A longitudinal study of school functioning in survivors of the Utøya shootings in 2011. *Eur J Psychotraumatol.* 2016; 7(10): 3402.

5   Sanohori, S. Veteran and Amputee Inspires with Each Death Defying Climb. *USA Today.* October 2018.

CHAPTER 16

1   Bloomer RJ, Kabir MM, Canale RE, et al. (2010). Effect of a 21 day Daniel Fast on metabolic and cardiovascular disease risk factors in men and women. *Lipids in health and disease.* 2010; 9(94). https://doi.org/10.1186/1476-511X-9-94.

2   Rico-Campà A, Martinez-González MA, Alvarez-Alvarez I, et al. Association between consumption of ultra-processed foods and all causes of mortality: SUN prospective cohort study. *British Medical Journal.* May 2019; 365.

3   Xu Y, Wang C, Klabnik JJ, O'Donnell JM. Novel therapeutic targets in depression and anxiety: Antioxidants as a candidate treatment. *Current neuropharmacology.* 2014; 12(2): 108–119.

4   Hilimire MR, DeVylder JE, Forestell CA. Fermented foods, neuroticism, and social anxiety: An interaction model. *Psychiatry Res.* 2015. August 15; 228(2): 203–08.

5   Baynham R, van Zanten J, Johns PW, et al. Cocoa flavored flavanols improve vascular response to acute mental stress in young healthy adults. *Nutrients.* 2021; 13(4): 1103.

6   An imbalance between production and accumulation of oxygen creating unstable molecules (free radicals), which cause cell damage.

7   Yuan C, Fondell E, Bhushan A, Ascherio A, Okereke OI, Grodstein F, Willett WC. Long-term intake of vegetables and fruits and subjective cognitive function in US men. *Neurology*. November 2018.

8   Ebenezer PJ, Wilson CB, Wilson LD, Nair AR, JF. The anti-inflammatory effects of blueberries in an animal model of post-traumatic stress disorder (PTSD). *PloS one*. 2016; 11(9).

9   Wanucha G. The gut microbiome and brain health: can we invite the right microbes into our gut to prevent Alzheimer's disease? *Dimensions*. Fall 2018.

10 Hoban AE, Stilling RM, Moloney GM, et al. Microbial regulation of microRNA expression in the amygdala and prefrontal cortex. *Microbiome*. 2017; 5, 102.

11 Cory H, Passarelli S, Szeto J, Tamez M, & Mattei J. The Role of Polyphenols in Human Health and Food Systems: A Mini-Review. *Frontiers in nutrition*. 2018; 5(87).

12 Parletta N, Zarnowiecki D, Cho J, et al. A Mediterranean-style diet intervention supplemented with fish oil improves diet quality and mental health in people with depression: A randomized controlled trial. Nutritional *Neuroscience*. Dec 2017; 474–487.

13 McEvoy CT, Hoang T, Sidney S, et al. Dietary patterns during adulthood and cognitive performance in midlife: The CARDIA study. *Neurology*. April 2019; 92(14).

14 Marinac CR, Nelson SH, Breen CI, et al. Prolonged nightly fasting and breast cancer prognosis. *JAMA Oncol*. 2016; 2, 1049–1055.

15 Longo Valter D, Mattson Mark P. Fasting: Molecular mechanisms and clinical applications. *Cell Metabolism*. 2014; 19(2): 181–92.

16 Faris MA, Kacimi S, Al-Kurd RA et al Intermittent fasting during Ramadan attenuates proinflammatory cytokines and immune cells in healthy subjects. *Nut Res*. 2012 Dec; 32(12): 947–55.

17 Feldman, A Everything you need to know about inflammation. *Medical News Today.com*. April; 2020.

18 Bhutani S, Klempel MC, Berger RA, Varady KA. Improvements in coronary heart disease risk indicators by alternate-day fasting

involve adipose tissue modulations. *Obesity*. 2010 Nov; 18(11): 2152–9.

19 Deuster PA, Kemmer T, Tubbs L et al. *The Special Operations Nutrition Guide*. US Department of Defense.

CHAPTER 17

1 Hunter MR, Gillespie BW, Chen S. Urban nature experiences reduce stress in the context of daily life based on salivary biomarkers. *Front. Psychol.* April 2019.

Index

About the Author

Tim Murphy, PhD, is a licensed psychologist specializing in resilience and recovery from psychological trauma.

Dr. Murphy served eight years as an officer in the US Navy Reserve, achieving the rank of Commander, was assigned to the staff in the inpatient Traumatic Brain Injury/PTSD unit at Walter Reed National Military Medical Center in Bethesda, MD, and held temporary assignments with the medical crew on three aircraft carriers, (USS Carl Vinson, USS Theodore Roosevelt, and USS Ronald Reagan) and with the assessment/selection team for with Navy Special Warfare. His awards include Joint Services Commendation, Navy Commendation with Gold Star, and Navy/Marine Achievement medal, among others.

Murphy was elected twice to the Pennsylvania State Senate and held the positions of chairman of the Aging and Youth Committee and vice chairman of Health and Welfare, and was a member of Appropriations, Banking/Insurance and Rules. While a senator, he authored the historic Managed Care Reform Act signed into law by Governor Tom Ridge.

Murphy was elected to the US House of Representatives eight times. Congressman Murphy was a member of the prestigious Committee on Energy and Commerce, chairman of the Subcommittee on Oversight and Investigation, cochairman of the Mental Health Caucus, chairman of the Steel Caucus, and founding cochairman of the Doctors' Caucus. He also was a member of the Financial Services Committee, and the Veterans Affairs

Committee. He authored and championed landmark mental health reforms while in Congress. After years of fighting for passage for his bill, the Helping Families in Mental Health Crisis Act of 2016 passed the house 422 to 2, was amended onto the 21st Century Cures act and signed into law in December 2016 by President Obama.

His many public-speaking appearances include hundreds of television and radio programs across the nation, academic conferences, universities and colleges in England and at military bases in the US and Okinawa, discussing mental health, trauma resilience, and public policy. He has authored numerous articles in academic journals, book chapters, editorials, trade magazines, web sites and blogs. Dr. Murphy is the coauthor of two books with Loriann Oberlin, *Overcoming Passive Aggression* (2009, 2nd ed. 2016) and *The Angry Child: Regaining Control When Your Child is Out of Control* (2001).

He received his PhD from the University of Pittsburgh, MA from Cleveland State University, and BA from Wheeling Jesuit University. Murphy also served on the staffs of Children's Hospital, and Mercy Hospital in Pittsburgh, and founded his own private practice. At the University of Pittsburgh, his faculty positions included assistant professor in the School of Medicine and adjunct assistant professor in the School of Public Health. He has been recognized as a champion for advocacy in mental health by the American Psychological Association, the American Psychiatric Association, the National Alliance on Mental Illness, Mental Health America, and many other national and state organizations.

Murphy is the founder and clinical director of Fortis Future (FortisFuture.com), located in suburban Pittsburgh, PA, a non-profit, multidisciplinary treatment program for veterans, military, and first responders coping with traumatic stress. Murphy also serves on boards and consults with national organizations advocating for improved treatment of mental illness and school safety.

He is married to Nanette, and they have a daughter (Bevin), son-in-law (Dan), and three beautiful grandchildren (Thomasina, Luca and Nico), all living in suburban Pittsburgh.

For more information about Tim Murphy, visit him at **LinkedIn: Tim Murphy PhD.**